PRAISE FOR
POETRY AS SPELLCASTING

"Reading *Poetry as Spellcasting*, I kept lighting my altar, kept nourishing my body with fragrant oranges as I dreamt, wandered, and envisioned. This is a book for *us*, for opening up the creative portals toward liberation, one tender prompt at a time. I felt held by these rituals and poems, felt myself move deeply into spaces of collective care. Alongside contributions from luminaries such as Alexis Pauline Gumbs, Joan Naviyuk Kane, and Ching-In Chen, the editors invoke magic through heart-igniting reflections and vibrational prompts, beautifully reminding us of our woven power: 'In this new mythology, you are always whole.'"

JANE WONG, author of *How to Not Be Afraid of Everything*

"Spellbinding, nourishing, and needed! *Poetry as Spellcasting* is unbounding and delivers a world of magic, incantations, and poetry for your spirit, skins, and memories to taste, discover, unfold, shed, and tend to the alchemy of our lives. Like rock candy or bubbles to the tongue, swallow and repeat to feel all your senses come alive, initiating a psychic surrender, embodiment, and deepening of why and how poets of color are casting spells for radically transformative, imaginative healing for our prayerful liberatory futures. Listen."

CARA PAGE, cofounder of Kindred Southern Healing Justice
Collective, founder of Changing Frequencies, and coauthor of
Healing Justice Lineages

"*Poetry as Spellcasting* is both alluring and substantive, gentle yet revolutionary. A provoking collection of poems and essays, this powerful book is sure to evoke inspiration, action, and reflection for readers."

MARIA MINNIS, author of *Anti-Racism with the Tarot*

T0273630

"*Poetry as Spellcasting* is an anthology I have been looking for all my writing life. Have you ever felt something so far from the 'norm' you just kept it to yourself? You talk to people with ancient names in a little place behind the eye(s), and you were once sure if anyone ever found out about this place, they would come and take you away, and you'll never see your mama again. *Poetry as Spellcasting* lets me know I am not alone in these southern Black ways of being. I keep thinking, what if my mama had this book when she was in high school? What kind of portal could it have been? *Poetry as Spellcasting* has set a new stage for what an anthology can be and how much it can do."

TYREE DAYE, author of *Cardinal*

"*Poetry as Spellcasting* gathers insightful and courageous provocations to affirm and amplify the world-shaping magics in our language. By our, I mean those of us laboring at the sites where devastation and (re)generation meet. By magics, I mean our capacities for care, transformation, and continuance. I received the spells in this book as gifts of renewal, as a summoning of the elements that activate our intentional presence, here and there, now and ever, among the countless trajectories of a hurting and beloved home-as-it-is-yet-to-be. The voices in this circle call me to pay closer attention, to commit to the discipline of repair, to begin again with grace."

CYNTHIA DEWI OKA, author of *Fire Is Not a Country*

"Alive, potent, and opening roads for and by multiple voices and beings, *Poetry as Spellcasting* is as much a work of art as a Spirit guidebook to our collective future. These are processes that embolden our purposes as healers and writers. The quiet space before anything is written lives here, echoes across time calling forth ways in the direction of our necessary un-doing for tomorrow. Grandmas, ritual sites, and plant medicine—all in poetry. *Poetry as Spellcasting* holds possibilities needed for our future, ways of writing that are not trapped, that go beyond the world as we have known it. Power is encapsulated in its most genuine and raw form. Power towards liberation for all beings. A holy, magical, unknowing that releases us into transcendence. These poem-makers invite all beings to stay, to imagine, to transcend, to transgress, to magic, and to make possible."

MARLANDA DEKINE, author of *Thresh & Hold*

POETRY AS SPELLCASTING

POEMS, ESSAYS, AND PROMPTS FOR MANIFESTING LIBERATION AND RECLAIMING POWER

Tamiko Beyer, Destiny Hemphill, and Lisbeth White

North Atlantic Books
Huichin, unceded Ohlone land
Berkeley, California

Published by
North Atlantic Books
Huichin, unceded Ohlone land
Berkeley, California

Cover images © knstartstudio via Shutterstock
Cover design by Emma Hall
Book design by Happenstance Type-O-Rama

Printed in Canada

Poetry as Spellcasting: Poems, Essays, and Prompts for Manifesting Liberation and Reclaiming Power is sponsored and published by North Atlantic Books, an educational nonprofit based in the unceded Ohlone land Huichin (Berkeley, CA) that collaborates with partners to develop cross-cultural perspectives, nurture holistic views of art, science, the humanities, and healing, and seed personal and global transformation by publishing work on the relationship of body, spirit, and nature.

North Atlantic Books's publications are distributed to the US trade and internationally by Penguin Random House Publisher Services. For further information, visit our website at www.northatlanticbooks.com.

Library of Congress Cataloging-in-Publication Data
Names: Beyer, Tamiko, author. | Hemphill, Destiny, author. | White, Lisbeth, 1979– author.
Title: Poetry as spellcasting : poems, essays, and prompts for manifesting liberation and reclaiming power / Tamiko Beyer, Destiny Hemphill, Lisbeth White.
Description: Berkeley, California : North Atlantic Books, [2023] | Summary: "Divided into four sections, Poetry as Spellcasting utilizes poetry as a tool for healing-justice transformation. The book guides readers to explore and deepen the creative and intuitive parts of themselves as catalysts for transformative healing and social change"— Provided by publisher.
Identifiers: LCCN 2022037448 (print) | LCCN 2022037449 (ebook) | ISBN 9781623177195 (trade paperback) | ISBN 9781623177201 (ebook)
Subjects: LCSH: Magic and poetry. | Poetics. | Poetry—Authorship. | Poetry—Social aspects. | Poetry—Political aspects. | Healing. | Social change. | LCGFT: Poetry. | Essays. | Problems and exercises.
Classification: LCC PN1077 .B49 2023 (print) | LCC PN1077 (ebook) | DDC 808.1—dc23/eng/20230118
LC record available at https://lccn.loc.gov/2022037448
LC ebook record available at https://lccn.loc.gov/2022037449

2 3 4 5 6 7 8 9 MARQUIS 28 27 26 25 24

This book includes recycled material and material from well-managed forests. North Atlantic Books is committed to the protection of our environment. We print on recycled paper whenever possible and partner with printers who strive to use environmentally responsible practices.

for us

CONTENTS

SUMMONING POWER AND CLOSING THE CIRCLE

OPENING THE CIRCLE

Awakening of Stones: Hypothesis/Central Argument

LISBETH WHITE

In the new mythology, you are always whole.
If and when you fracture, it is not apart.
Apart does not exist here.

You will know that upon entry.
You will know each fissure as it breaks open your life.
You will know the cracked edges of your splendor.
You will know the steady tear and repair of your muscles.
It is true. The work is letting go while pulling back together.
It is true. The heart is broken less by pain, more often
by the beauty we fear we cannot offer.

You are born knowing how to make the sounds of your heart.
You are born knowing how to make your hands into wings.

how we got our blues-tongue

DESTINY HEMPHILL

after The Commodores and Tramaine Hawkins & with a line from Toni Cade Bambara

& the augurs among us direct our gaze to the sky all alluvial

breaking through, breaking blue & we open our mouths to

catch the cerulean, catch the rugged blues again on our tongue, blurred &
    bruised

decadent deluge of dirge drenching skin, dandelions, & dirt. diviners say we
    dancing dizzy to the

ends of the world, dancing at the end of the world. to elsewhere. edging to

flight. let there be flight. & there flight be. we be a many-forked tongue folk

glossolalia-gurgling, crossing- & -translating- other-realms folk. apocalyptic
    glitch, we put our

hands on our hips, then put our hands in the air, hold our hands to the haints
    & catch their

iridescent feathers. oh haints, come true to us, come blue to us, come through
    to this

juke joint we call earth, this jagged jollification. we won't jilt you. no, we

keep our dead kin with us as the dead kin have kept us the living.

listen, empire can't catch us. but it can catch these hands of redistribution,
    these

moonfire spells to undo & redo, these fractalwinged myths exploding the
    means, this

newness, this emergence—that isn't actually that new at all. if we telling the
    truth about our

origins, this is quite old. blues old, which is bones old, which is dirt old. oh,
    yes we've got our

poems, parables, psalms, & our own palms as record that we've refashioned
    ourselves before, we've

questioned ourselves before. quivered with loss before. made portal of crisis &
    quantum leap-

rebirthed. bled & tended flesh wounds with rest & stinging medicine before
    because the material without the

spiritual & psychic does not a dialectic make. let's get the rhythm of our feet,
    let's get the rhythm of our

throats, holding a cosmic alchemy of tragedy & celebration that can turn this
    thing

upside down so that the sky becomes soil & soil becomes sky & dirt is what
    we seek for salvation.

verily, verily, when you get this rhythm, meet us at the crossroads. you'll know
    because you'll hear

whistling from the mulberry trees. you'll smell them, too. & we'll be there,
    perched. looking real

xenial & otherworldly. we'll be humming with the haints, conspiring about
    going up

yonder. going up yonder to be with our motherworld.

zoom zoom. we'd like to fly away. fly away to right here.

February

TAMIKO BEYER

I'm climbing out of this season, fingernails ragged, belly soft. I tuck a stem of dried mint behind my ear to remind myself.

Once, I bared my shoulders. The bottom of my feet roughed up the dirt with calluses. When I harvested arugula, it smelled of green—alchemical veins pulsing sun and dirt and water. I do remember this. I pinned summer light up in my hair and made no apologies for the space I took up—barely clothed and sun-bound.

Now, a ball of twine in the grey sky. The sun rolls low on the horizon. Hangs. Then dips back down again, wind howling us into night.

Inside the erratic rhythm of this wavering flame, I conjure the potent sky of the longest day. Seeds with a whole galaxy inside. Cicadas vibrating in alders.

But the sensation of joy slips too quickly into simulacra. Song on repeat. I never meant to find myself in such a cold place, my hair thinning against winter.

Once, red clover grew thick where today's rabbit tracks pattern the snow. Clover said flow, clover said nourish, clover said we've got this.

I reel the memory out, let it linger on the horizon, then reel it back in. I play it out and reel it back in. Some kind of fishing, some kind of flying—again and again. I loosen the buckles of my mind. I take up space in the precision of my breath. I call us all back in.

Introduction

In 2018, the Supreme Court upheld the forty-fifth president's "Muslim ban" in *Trump* v. *Hawaii*. At the same time, it overruled the 1944 decision that justified the imprisonment of more than 120,000 Japanese and Japanese American people during World War II. Poet Kenji C. Liu put out a call for spells that responded to this judicial "sleight of hand," as he phrased it, and to the imprisonment of thousands of children and families by ICE. He gathered fourteen poem-spells written by poets of color in a folio for the online journal *Unmargin*. In his introduction, he wrote:

> *In addition to protesting, building complex communities of resistance and vision, and self-care practices, writers also have language, one of the original magicks. We too can summon our own enchantments, incantations, protections, charms, curses, hexes, blessings, auguries, banishments, and more.*

These words planted a seed in Tamiko Beyer's mind, which sprouted into a panel on "Poetry as Spellcasting" offered at the 2019 &Now conference at the University of Washington, Bothell. Beyer, Destiny Hemphill, Lisbeth White, and Tatiana Figueroa Ramirez—all of us poets with a variety of relationships to and experiences with ritual and spellcasting—led a writing ritual. It ended with the two dozen or so participants standing in a circle, casting a collective spell for liberation and transformation. We felt the energy swirl between us, through the room, and out to where we were sending our intentions: an ICE detention center several miles away. In that place, in that moment, the concept of poetry-as-spellcasting blossomed from a seedling into a lush and powerful being unto itself.

A different configuration of poet-spellcasters, Beyer, Figueroa Ramirez, Liu, and Sun Yung Shin, prepared and led a similar panel at the annual writers' conference known as AWP in March 2020. In the last packed room that many of us would step into for the next two years, we cast another powerful collective spell for liberation and transformation. Shortly after, we were invited by North Atlantic Books to turn our thinking and spellcasting into book form.

Over the next two years, editors Beyer, Hemphill, and White dreamed into poetry as spellcasting. We reached out to our networks, we edited, and we wrote. We moved at the pace of Life, bringing this book into being in the midst of a global pandemic, uprisings for racial justice, mass shootings, an attempted coup, a sharpening climate crisis, economic precarity, personal crises, travels, and disruptions. We met over video conference, often on full and new moons, connecting across the country to work, laugh, rage, write, puzzle through challenges, and honor the unnamable mystery of poetry as spellcasting.

And finally, here we are. This book in itself is a spell, a sea-serpent, a seedling grown to a fruit-bearing tree. It is the result of a deeply collaborative process between the three of us, in which we also asked for and received contributions and energies from a whole web of other writers. Together, we cowrote sections, and we also contributed essays and poems individually.

The result is part anthology, part poetry collection, part workbook. We asked just a few of our friends and writers we admired to contribute specific essays on poetry as spellcasting, based on what we knew of their work. We were delighted and surprised by the direction they went with the topic. We wove these essays, along with prompts and poems by us and others, to create a body of work that we hope will be accessible in many different ways. There were many more writers and witches we would have loved to include if we had unlimited time and space, and we hope this book might plant a seed, the way Liu's folio did, for other manifestations of poetry as spellcasting.

The three of us identify variously as Black, multiracial, Asian American, disabled, queer, and femme. We wrote and edited this book as a love poem and spell by and for poets of color, spellmakers, magic makers. We conceived of the book as queer, bringing a queer investigation into our practices. For us, poetry and ritual are not separate from the larger political landscape in which we live, write, and cast spells.

Indeed, language has the power to both reflect and manifest our shared perceptions of reality and the world in which we live. Human language is transmitted socially, yet the words we speak and write begin in the most intimate and most uniquely creative corners of our psyches. What we think and believe lives in internal language before (and regardless of whether) we utter a word. We know that it benefits systems that wish to stay in power to control our access to certain languages as soon as possible. Imperialistic, human-centric, colonial, racist, cissexist, heteronormative, consumer-capitalist, patriarchal, ableist—these are all types of language that are embedded in educational systems, workplaces, religious settings, and even homes, aimed to constrict the ways we name and understand the world as we know it.

And yet—while human language, like any human construction, is susceptible to institutional and cultural capture and violence, there is something about language that is serpent-like: fluid, potent, capable of slipping through tight spaces and recreating itself like new skin. Here is where poetry and spellcasting converge.

Even as scholarship and discipline hone skillful application of both, poetry and the magical arts have long been practices of the people. Like nearly all arts, they arose organically in human life, accessible to any and all seeking to explore relationships to such practices, despite attempts to colonize and isolate this access. Most practitioners of poetry, ritual, or any creative endeavor will express moments of opening or surrender to an energy that feels beyond the personal ego—a something mighty and unnamed. As both poetry and spellcasting exist and play in the spaces closest to this mystery, they offer us ways to enter into and harness language in a heightened way as tools to both disrupt and manifest.

To that end, and bowing to the serpentine nature of language, we want here to offer brief definitions of *poetry, spellcasting,* and *ritual,* which we use throughout the book. By *poetry* we mean works of art where the instrument is language, where as much is left unsaid as said. We mean a form that uses imagery, metaphor, the musicality of language, and often brevity to convey both meaning and emotional weight. By *spellcasting,* we mean a direction of intention and energy to call in forces beyond ourselves: spiritual, ancestral, and earthly allies. We conceive of spellcasting as a concentration and alignment of energy and language in a ritual. And by *ritual,* we mean putting our bodies into ceremony or practice as a means of understanding and encountering different knowings and forces beyond what is easily available to most of us outside of the ritual space.

These are our definitions, in this moment, in this context. You probably have your own definitions, which we invite you to integrate into what you encounter here. In the end, our aim is to offer to you ideas, tools, and prompts that may help you harness the revolutionary, transformative, and liberatory potential of poetry as spellcasting.

We have opened with poetry from the three editors and a ritual for setting the space. This is followed by six sections that each include two essays, a related prompt, and a poem.

In "Portals of Inheritance: Ancestral Teachings, Possible Futures," the essays of Alexis Pauline Gumbs and Laurin DeChae along with Destiny Hemphill's poem and the related prompt open portals to messages from ancestors and for survival. In "Languages of Liberation, Disruption, and Magic," Kenji C. Liu, Dominique Matti, and Lisbeth White explore the magic potent in language and in nature. Their essays and poems along with the related prompt offer opportunities to step into, learn from, and be transformed by the power of language and magic.

In "Invoking Radical Imagination," White and Hyejung Kook take two very different approaches to leaning into the incantatory possibilities of poetry as prayer and poetry as enchantment, while the related prompt invites you into an experience of reenchantment. The section "Sacred Practices: Rituals of Repair and Revision" encourages considerations of how the practices of repetition, return, and revision create sacred spaces and movements toward transformation. It features essays from Amir Rabiyah and Tamiko Beyer, as well as a poem from Tatiana Figueroa Ramirez.

From there, we move to confluence of magical practices and sociopolitical intentions in poetry as spellcasting. "Lighting Fires, Breaking Chains" features excerpts from an essay by Lou Florez interwoven with an interview conducted with Florez by Beyer and White, and a poem by Ching-In Chen. In "Elemental Ecologies, Spiritual Technologies," the essays of Joan Naviyuk Kane and Sun Yung Shin and a poem by Beyer wrestle with concepts of home, colonization, belonging, and ways poetry can offer us paths toward survival, connection to the earth, and deeper relationship with our more-than-human kin.

We close with "Summoning Power and Closing the Circle." Hemphill's essay charges us to listen closely and evoke the liberatory power of poetry as spellcasting. "Wander, Weave, (Un)know, Re-member," cowritten by all three editors, reflects back what we have learned from these pages and calls the reader to take this work out into the world. Our aim is that the final poem—crafted out of lines you'll encounter throughout the book—and the closing ritual will assist you in integrating the whisperings, shouts, and spells contained here.

With its capacity to both build and break through, language in these pages moves like the serpent, embodying qualities of innovation and resurgence. It is in this innovation that possibility toward liberation is activated. In naming the world with imagination and creativity, we come to understand that the harmful structures of society must change. This naming and understanding pose both a great threat to the status quo and a great invitation to transformation.

Our hope is that this book will inspire you to play, experiment with, and practice the transformative art of poetry as spellcasting. We invite you to engage with it in the way you most feel called to do so. Perhaps you will travel through the book in a linear fashion, or you will dip in and out of sections. You might try opening it at random and see what invites your attention on any day. The prompts can be done as you read each chapter, or on their own. However you engage with it, it is the right way.

This is how we have approached the crafting of *Poetry As Spellcasting:* listening to our intuition, to each other, and to the spirits who have guided us along the way. It has been an enormous joy and pleasure to work together to bring this being into the world. We hope that you find as much magic and love in reading it as we did in its creation.

RITUAL FOR SETTING THE SPACE

★ Throughout this book, there will be invitations to engage in writing exercises and rituals to help you deepen and integrate tools for poetry and spellcraft. We're offering this first ritual as a supportive container for you to return to as you work your way through the essays and exercises. The steps below will help you create a sacred space to visit before, during, or after you write, as a way to connect with your power, your intentions, and your intuition.

★ Find a space where you can set up a small altar. It can be a corner of a room, a windowsill, a table or dresser top—whatever feels accessible. Clean the space and dress it with some fabric, a plant, or anything that feels welcoming.

★ Place on the altar an object that reminds you of your power or times when you feel a sense of power. This could be a stone, a photograph, a candle, a memento—anything that evokes power for you.

★ Place on the altar an object that helps you feel connected to your intuition. This can be anything that evokes a sense of connection to your deep knowing.

★ Finally, place on the altar an object that helps you feel connected to the people, beings, or communities that are most important to you.

★ Invite the elements into the space. You can do this by lighting a candle (fire); bringing a glass of water (water); placing a feather if you have one, speaking a word, or gently blowing on to the altar (air); placing a stone, crystal, or a small bowl of dirt on the altar (earth).

★ Intentionally visit this space for ten days. Take a few moments to sit and take in the objects and the feel of the altar. Then free-write for ten to thirty minutes.

★ After the ten days, reflect on what it felt like to return to the space daily. What unfurled? What contracted? What felt obstructed? What flowed? This could take the form of a journal entry, meditation, or poem.

★ Return to this space and this initial writing any time you wish.

PORTALS OF INHERITANCE:
Ancestral Teachings, Possible Futures

Survival Radio

ALEXIS PAULINE GUMBS

For Audre and Genevieve

we were never meant to
—AUDRE LORDE, "A LITANY FOR SURVIVAL"

I.

Radio waves will be here long after we all are gone.

In phases, everything we built to support our lives will crumble. Nature will reclaim what we are currently stealing. Plants and animals or whatever organisms survive and emerge out of our changes to the climate will vine through and grow and propagate like what we see happening now in the empty-of-people (but not empty at all) city of Chernobyl. Or at least that's what Alan Weisman says in *The World Without Us,* which tracks what would happen on this planet if humans completely disappeared.

But the radio waves. They will continue to move out into the expanding universe, unbound by the lost infrastructure of cities and the towers that were once their relay stations—far into space, until they are drowned out by the louder cosmic noise of—what? The next universe creating itself? What can receive all that afterlife of vibration as vibration? Someone trying to say something. A voice longing over longer and longer distances to be heard.

That's what I'm sitting here doing, in 2020 as the world falls apart and indeed humans disappear a little bit, but not enough, from the cities we built to bear our weight. I am trying to learn how to receive the longing of an expanding universe. Since domination, extraction, and consumption are what keep us speeding toward our own disappearance, I am desperate for another form of reception. Could I listen deeper, tune into another possibility beyond the sad apocalyptic jingle that is swift becoming the legacy of our species?

I call it survival radio. This practice where I pull what I need out of the air and hope to vibrate differently. Breathe back frequencies that hold, that slow us down, that move us through, beyond the bounce of feedback.

Maybe Black feminist lesbian poet warrior Audre Lorde would have called this practice a séance, like the ones she had with her high school girlfriends before homeroom, listening for dead romantic poets, the only references they could find who were as dramatic as teenagers.

Lucille Clifton might have called it a regular school night as a mother raising six children. She pulled out the toy-store Ouija board to get useful messages from her dead mother. That same practice eventually led to hundreds of unpublished (and according to her correspondence unpublish*able*) messages from ghosts as varied as Bonnie and Clyde and Frederick Douglass. Her practice of listening to the air resulted in her haunting and helpful "message from the ones."

Or is it more like what Trinidadian lawyer turned Afro-Canadian poet M. NourbeSe Philip did with her book *Zong:* a breath deep enough to catch the prayers of the drowning enslaved captives whom the owners of the eponymous ship threw off the boat intentionally? Philip refracted their last breaths against the words of the legal battle for an insurance claim against their chatteled lives.

Toni Cade Bambara might have referred to this same practice as an alignment of scale, putting her hands above her head and pulling down ideas like she did standing in a circle of sisters (including Clifton and Philip, by the way) at the 1988 *Essence* magazine Black Women Writers Retreat in Nassau, Bahamas. She was explaining that the writers gathered there should put together an anthology, not just of position papers like her 1970 *The Black Woman*, but also poems, recipes, legislative proceedings, and star maps.

Maybe I'm not just pulling it out of the air after all. Maybe this is just what Black feminist writers do.

II.

Audre Lorde, Black feminist lesbian icon, quoted on T-shirts and organizational websites, has become a marker for a complex understanding of identity, multiplicity, and intersectionality. Her work to emphasize "the creative power of difference" in the spaces where she lived and worked through most of the second half of the twentieth century have been crucial for the feminist, LGBTQ, and Black liberation movements. But I am invoking a different Audre. Not the icon, but the teen. Before she was able to claim any of the legibly different identities we seek to honor when we call her name. I call on the Audre who was just weird. A high school student who didn't know how to say the things she most wanted to say. Not the silence-breaking voice she became, but the girl who, as she explained in an interview with fellow poet Adrienne Rich, was trained in her strict West Indian mother's house to navigate the unsaid by intuition, evading the risk of speech. I can relate. In fact, that's who I was when I first started reading Audre Lorde. Now, as a vibrational practice, I want to listen for that particular Audre, turn the dial through the static over to the Audre Lorde of 1948, having the best and scariest summer of her life with her suicidal best friend and first love, Genevieve.

Why? Because I don't know if I would have survived high school without Audre Lorde. I cannot underestimate the value of having the purple bible of her collected poetry and using it again and again for the epigraphs of everything I wrote when I was a teenager. This is what I wonder when people like me testify over and over to how Audre Lorde saved our lives, and even more every time we lose a young queer person of color to suicide: *How did Audre Lorde survive high school without her own Audre Lorde, her own epic precedent to make Black queer life feel possible?*

One way to answer that question is to say she almost didn't. This is what she leads us to know in the biomythography *Zami*. Her best friend and first love killed herself. The rest of her friends voluntarily got to school early to listen for the dead in makeshift seances. What if it had been Audre who took her own life in the drama and desperation of high school in the 1940s, when the word "teenager" had just come into popular usage and the word "homosexual" was being weaponized in the McCarthy witch hunts? Would her best friend, the brave Black ballet dancer Genevieve, be the icon we used as our crossroads to difference? Or would all that path-making just never have happened? Where would I be, where would you be, then?

Or maybe Audre Lorde did not survive high school without Audre Lorde. She survived *as* Audre Lorde. Becoming Audre Lorde. With Audre Lorde. Present to herself. It is a major part of my life's work to study the survival technologies of Audre Lorde, and don't you want to know how she did it? I want to time travel to Audre Lorde's high school years and know for sure what broke Genevieve's spirit. What allowed Audre to endure. The love between them. The difference between them.

And though the quantity may be different, after years of research, what I have is what I had in high school. Audre Lorde's words. And too much longing. On the margins of an essay she was writing, Audre Lorde wrote "I love the word survival. It sounds to me like a promise." I believe that survival is important, not because we need the bare minimum, but because we do the most and we deserve so much more. We deserve survival, a word that honors the continued ancestral presence of those people we are supposedly living without. We deserve survival, a spell that points to the triumph of our existence in disaster circumstances. Because we were never meant to.

III.

If you survive, you get to tell the story. So my portal back to summer 1948 and 1949 is Audre Lorde's literary memory, documented decades after Genevieve died in the pages of her biomythography *Zami* and in the poems that she wrote and rewrote throughout her life about grieving her lost friend. Aided by Lorde's more immediate memories documented in her journals, which recount longings, ideas, and angst, but not many details about the daily living she did with Genevieve while she was dying inside.

Zami, Audre Lorde's biomythography, which she wrote specifically to answer a challenge by Barbara Smith, to show that it was in fact possible to "be a Black lesbian feminist writer and live to tell about it," is not a memoir. Audre Lorde herself related to it as a novel. In public readings from the book she referred to "the novel" and "the main character" to let us know that she was navigating what she would later call "the marvelous arithmetics of distance." She offers a step back from her own life in order to offer readers intimacy with the magic of loving women that she said kept her alive. I read *Zami* less as an archive of facts and more as a treasure map telling me what Audre the writer found most resonant and useful in her own refracted memories. Here I tune in to the impossibilities and discrepancies that show up in *Zami*.

IV.

For example, Audre Lorde says that the two girls would listen to Genevieve's grandmother's Nat King Cole albums, specifically the song "Dance, Ballerina, Dance," a sad song in which the crooning narrator describes a heartbroken ballerina who has chosen her art over the offer of love. This song is especially appropriate for Genevieve's situation. She too must "ignore [her] aching heart" when she performs. When she looks out into the audience, "he isn't there applauding in the second row." The "he" is not a former lover, but her father who has been absent from her life and who continues to disappoint after she goes to live with him. But the girls could not have heard this song on a Nat King Cole record borrowed from Genevieve's grandmother when they were in high school. Nat King Cole did not record this song until 1957, six years after Genevieve died.

So what is possible? The song itself *was* around when the girls were in high school, sung by two prominent white singers during Audre and Genevieve's early high school years. Maybe it was a song Genevieve favored, and later, when Audre Lorde heard the Nat King Cole version, she would think of Genevieve's sadness.

Alternately, and this is a long shot, maybe they did hear Nat King Cole sing this song. The Nat King Cole trio had a radio show while the girls were in high school. Could he have sung "Dance, Ballerina, Dance" on the radio years before he recorded it?

Or maybe the song simply speaks so precisely to the felt memory of Genevieve that when it did come out in 1957, Audre Lorde began to relate to it as the soundtrack to those memories of her high school best friend.

I find it evocative and appropriate that impossible outcomes occur in *Zami*, especially in this section, because the proliferation of possibility is core to how Lorde describes Genevieve's life. We know she must have gone over other possibilities in her mind, imagined a version of the story where both she and Genevieve graduate high school, and dance to Nat King Cole in 1957 and beyond.

That is not what happened. What happened is that Genevieve tried to kill herself, twice—at least two times that Audre knew about in advance. All summer Genevieve explained that she was going to kill herself before school started back up. And in *Zami*, when Audre asks, "What about all of us who love you," Genevieve brushes it off and Audre feels dumb for asking. So she doesn't bring it up again. In *Zami*, Genevieve's grandmother, the one with the records, found Genevieve in a tub full of blood. She had slit her wrists. From the hospital Genevieve called Audre and bemoaned her failure. Audre privately rejoiced. Genevieve's mother relented and let her go live with her father. It wasn't a good situation. One night, Genevieve came over with visible scratches, and Audre lied to her mother and said she was just asking about homework even though in the narrative of *Zami* Audre and Genevieve didn't even go to the same school anymore now that she lived with her father. Genevieve asked if she could stay. Audre was afraid to ask her already suspicious and strict mother. So Genevieve left and rode the train all night and ate fifteen capsules of rat poison. One for every year of her life. And this time she didn't fail. She died a few days later. Audre Lorde survived, determined to teach the world, and especially Black women, about the costs of silence.

V.

And the possibilities of voice. In *Zami*, the day that Audre finds out that Genevieve is dead from her second suicidal action, she describes herself as hearing Sarah Vaughan singing Genevieve's favorite song, "Harbor Lights," stuck on repeat over in a local store until the clerk kicks the jukebox. This is also the perfect image. Troubled Genevieve would love this melancholy song, and for the young Audre, the scene where a woman watches the lights of a boat that is taking her lover across an ocean she cannot navigate, would resonate deeply. The problem is there is no recording of Sarah Vaughan singing "Harbor Lights." But like the Nat King Cole Trio, Sarah Vaughan also had a fifteen-minute radio show while Audre and Genevieve were in high school. Maybe they heard that one night during their Wednesday–Sunday schedule; maybe they sang it more than once, even, and Genevieve favored it. It could be possible that by an eerie coincidence Audre heard Sarah Vaughan singing the song again live if the store had a radio instead of or in addition to the jukebox. But the show was Wednesday, Thursday, and Friday, and Genevieve died on a Tuesday. Jukeboxes were just coming back into availability after production on them had been halted to divert materials to weaponry for World War II.

It is much more likely that if "Harbor Lights" was Genevieve's favorite, she heard Dinah Washington's rendition, which was recorded in the late 1940s while the girls were in high school and circulated enough to be part of Washington's rise to become the most popular jazz singer of the next decade. No one could mistake the edge in Dinah Washington's voice for Sarah Vaughan's suave, but the two singers were born the same year and started their careers close to the same time. Both would have been visible and audible to Audre and Genevieve as famous singers during the last great years of radio, before the distributions of televisions. And maybe Genevieve preferred Sarah

Vaughan. Or maybe Audre Lorde wrote it that way because while Dinah Washington died at thirty-nine, not so many years after Genevieve's own death, Sarah Vaughan lived on. Vaughan was still alive and singing when Audre Lorde was writing *Zami.* Maybe it would have been better if Sarah was Genevieve's favorite; maybe Genevieve really loved Dinah. We do not know. If in *Zami* Audre Lorde had the power to go back and change one small thing, the singer on the record, one small thing, the year the song came out, one small thing, the glitches of a jukebox, maybe she could go back and change what she really wanted to change, just a small change, a change of quantity. Not one but two black girls live.

I like to imagine Genevieve hearing Dinah Washington singing Clyde Otis's "This Bitter Earth." It epitomizes Genevieve's sadness, which lives now in my own heart thanks to Lorde. I'm not listening to the version recorded almost a decade after Genevieve died. I'm playing the 2018 version on Max Richter's "The Blue Notebooks" remastered over his composition "On the Nature of Daylight." I see Genevieve dancing to that version. Not young and troubled, but old and wise, the hurt and brilliant girl who survived, not only in the poems and fictionalized memories of her best friend but in muscle, reach, and embodied meaning. That's the impossible possibility I want. A whole life sustained by one small change.

Throughout her life, Audre Lorde wrote poems about Genevieve. A series of poems titled "Memorial" with Roman numerals behind them. In these poems we hear Lorde begging for communication from her dead friend. She rushes into phone booths, watches birds, sits on a favorite bench, scours her dreams, and does revisionist readings of weather reports. Poems have to do what existing telecommunications systems cannot, but over and over again Lorde seeks out these wired and wireless systems, as if in hope that this time the connection will be slightly different, different enough that she will hear Genevieve's voice. At the end of her life in *Undersong,* her book of revisions of her own poems, Lorde practiced the art of the small change. Most notably adding spaces not between, but *within* poetic lines. For example, from "Memorial II":

> Genevieve tell me

becomes

> Genevieve   tell me

and

> far from me even

becomes

> far from me   even

A space for Genevieve's answer? A shift toward acknowledging absence? A granting of emotional space?

For me, poetry *is* the practice of small changes. Not only in its revision, but all along. Placing words together with differences that are slight, but meaningful. We invite poetry readers to participate in the possibility of a small change by leaving enough ambiguity in our spacing that the poem could be read multiple ways out loud, interpreted differently by which words lean together in your mouth. My poetry understands rhythm and rhyme as the reinvocation of the same moment over and over again but with an incremental difference that means everything. Holding the ethical imperative that Lucille Clifton taught her poetry students, the possibility of "saying the right thing, at the right time, to the right person."

VI.

It only took a month of me writing this to follow Audre Lorde's instructions. *I'm doing my work,* she says, *are you doing yours?* What do I want to change? Where is my Black girl heartbreak? Right here:

> *Dear Ai Elo,*
>
> *I miss you. Every time I share those pictures of us at the Combahee River on the 150th Anniversary of Harriet Tubman's uprising, I think about your triumph. I didn't know that it was a triumph, that instant, the first weekend I met you. How unlikely that you would have survived high school. But it was a triumph. Wasn't it?*

It wasn't until we were singing with you for the Many Voices video, the sacred space that Katina Parker curated to reclaim Black Queer Spirituality, that I realized the depth of homophobia you experienced in church and at home growing up. I didn't know on that first trip, how much it must have meant to you later that same river baptism day when the pastor welcomed us to the front of that small church, wearing all white, drenched in Tubman's legacy. Did you feel saved? Did you think you had already saved your own life?

When I found out about your first suicide attempt the next year, not necessarily the very first, but the first since I knew you, I was so grateful that you failed. That you lived. I thought the community we built had helped save you. You felt loved enough to call for help, and we answered.

When Audre Lorde's best friend's first suicide attempt failed, she was grateful too. In Zami *she said she decided to stop stealing the Sunday School money her mother gave her. It helped Audre's own relationship with God. For a moment.*

Your survival helped me believe more in community. As a person who never *let community know I was struggling* ever, *as the daughter, granddaughter, and great-granddaughter of women who struggled with neurodivergence and crisis without robust, responsive, let alone queer Black feminist community to call on, your survival, your call, and our answer made me feel something was possible beyond what I had known.*

But I didn't think about suicidal ideation as progressive, or the experience of survival as instructive, not in how to survive, but how to kill yourself better, more quickly with less space for intervention the next time.

You know, you answered my call. My first call to go on the pilgrimage to Combahee. And I remember at the bus station you said it felt too good to be true. You wondered if it was a scam to get your money. And I said I wish. I wish that Black feminism was popular enough that someone would even think to use it as a get-rich-quick scheme. *Right now that wish seems more possible than it was then. Partially because of us.*

So maybe you did give me the clue that you were someone who had been deeply hurt and lied to about something very important. They told you, the people who made you, that God hated you. They told you and made you repeat it back. They somehow kept you alive with that poison, so how could you know it from food?

But this instant, this triumph, you did somehow sense that it was a lie. You did. And you became a poet. A famous champion youth slam poet. When did you first read Audre Lorde? Did you change the spelling of your name so your folks wouldn't know what you were screaming from the stage?

Sister genius, I found a video from when you were in high school in the Brave New Voices competition under a different name than the one I knew you by. Sheliel, woman of God. You were shouting, reciting a poem about a woman who killed her own babies because she thought it would be better than suffering in poverty here on this bitter earth. Was it a call for help? And who answered? What happened to your mother that your grandmother raised you with such tightness and fear? What do you say in that nobody's-fault-but-mine Many Voices video where you explain that you are starting to pray again, how your grandmother taught you how to pray? Audre prayed for Genevieve. And loved her harder.

And yet, those of us who love you couldn't hold your life in our hands. Only you could. And life was heavy to hold, expensive to support as a poet. You lived in the homes of family members who couldn't love you unconditionally. Who thought your queerness was a condition of sin. Your aunt did pay for you to come on the pilgrimage, though. What would it have taken for you to know and feel, not in your brain but in your gut and your hands, that God loved you. That we all loved you. That you would have had your pick of guest beds and couches from here to Black feminist eternity, coast to coast.

If I was more at home with myself, could I have made you feel more at home? Sometimes I thought you were asking for too much at the retreat—different food, less incense, the keys to the building. You accidentally locked us all out of the building where we were staying at some point, and I was pissed. But I tried not to show it. I said, you can do it. Call this number. Get us back inside. *I didn't know how deeply wrong you felt, and I was triggered by the reflection of myself I saw in you. Too much like me, so I kept you at arms distance. A wide embrace with space for the part of myself I feared would somehow ask for too much. The rejection I feared. I held something back. Was it the refuge that you needed?*

I still almost never call for help. I protect myself from what would save me. I defend the right to inflict pain, deprival, and isolation on my ownself. Is that why I couldn't embrace you better, closer, realer? Because I would have had to learn that on myself? Ai Elo. I'm sorry. I love you. Please forgive me. I am still learning. Is it wrong to learn from your death how to love myself better? But now I have to. It's the one thing I can change.

Love,
Alexis

WRITING TO YOUR ABSENT PRESENCE

The epistolary form, or letter-writing, can be a meaningful practice to contact grief or longing as you reach toward an absent presence.

★ Begin by resting your hand or your thoughts over your heart. Breathe into your heartspace five clarifying breaths. Whom or what have you been missing lately?

★ When you are ready, grab whatever you like to write with.

★ Write a letter to an absent presence—your knowing and not-knowing, your here and not-here, your not-here but felt, what-is-here-in-your-heart but not-out-there-in-the-world-in-the-same-way. This could be a person, a place, an ideal, a previous version of yourself, a desire, or something else altogether.

★ In your letter, share with your absent presence what your love of them and grief for them have made possible. How has the way that you relate to versions of your past, present, and future been transformed through your love and grief?

★ Put the letter in a sacred space—your altar, your bedside table, your kitchen counter, your favorite book, whatever sacred looks like for you—for three days.

★ On the fourth day, read it, and then write a letter or poem back to yourself and the places that your grief or longing resides within you. These places could be places in your body that you feel grief or longing most strongly—your hands, throat, behind your knees, your heart, gut, or somewhere else.

★ Put both letters or poems in a sacred space for another three days.

★ On the seventh day, read both of your letters or poems. Give an offering of thanks. And then let them go—recycle them, compost them, shred them, burn them, or bury them in the ground and water them.

I Am

LAURIN DECHAE

Above all else, the larger scope of my dissertation project examines the ways in which Black women have continuously created a blueprint, through art, literature, activism, and especially the mundane, for healing and restorative practices under some of the most enduring systemic conditions that undermine the very definition of humanity. How, when saddled with the grotesqueries of being the mule of the world, we stood firm in the sound of our own names. This is an exercise in surrendering as a means of healing wounds, both old and new. Throughout, I consider the ways in which inter- and intragenerational traumas shape how we perceive and are perceived by the world around us and, as such, collage a world of magic that is both volatile and wondrous. This is a project of both/and, requiring a kind of simultaneity in the sense that its end goal is an investigation of the self as a means of integrating, rather than purging, our multiplicities. It asks not, what must survive and what must fall away, but rather, what would it mean to live prismatically?

With a particular eye toward assemblage, each of the twelve sections utilizes a zodiac affirmation statement and the corresponding universal law as focal points for the rest of the material to orbit around. It troubles the waters in an attempt to make spells, poetry, meditation, scholarship, astrology, hoodoo, and popular culture meet in the middle like an asterisk. Here, I encode both road opening and honey jar spells in pages that are meant to resemble a kind of grimoire. The pages were fed with coffee, rum, and homemade florida water. They sat on the altar of my ancestors with candles aflame. They are magic because I am magic.

In the first section of the project, excerpted here, the twinned aspects of the Aries affirmation, "I am," and the first universal law of divine oneness work to create a map that helps us return back to the essence of who we are regardless of the cultural or societal baggage we've picked up along the way. Regardless of the lies that refuse us power. It is a spell of active self-definition that recognizes oneness as collective consciousness—polyvocality—and the ways in which we are connected to each other and the material world. *Everything is everything.* The ways we are made of matter. The assertion that we do matter. Aside from this there are two other primary frames for this section: Alexis Pauline Gumbs's book *Spill: Black Feminist Scenes of Fugitivity* alongside Misha Green's seventh episode of *Lovecraft Country* titled "I Am." The alignment here is intended to juxtapose limitations of movement and definition as we work toward authentic liberation and liberatory practices. It is an Afrofuturist enfolding of past, present, and future moments that synthesize, in many ways, those things both personal and political that I had been unable to articulate up until this point.

As such, this first section is a spell of mapping by way of biomythography. How we shape our mouths to speak in chorus in whichever words we choose. In the tarot, Aries is represented by the Emperor card, and this section asks us, what would it mean to have authority over self, to be the creator of our own worlds? How do we understand universality from Black women's perspectives? As it is written in the Combahee River Collective Statement, "If Black women were free, it would mean that everyone else would have to be free since our freedom would necessitate the destruction of all the systems of oppression." This is a spell with instructions on being a verb rather than a noun, opening up paths toward freedom, and how to be sweet to yourself once you get there.

I Am: Biomythography, Self-Definition, and the Law of Oneness

with lines from Alexis Pauline Gumbs' *Spill: Scenes of Black Feminist Fugitivity*

once the ancestor stars were not just night lights to wish upon

it was about the same sad thing unsaid across generations

the seed / the sprout / the wilt

and all that passes in between

"I am myself struggling toward myself"
—"The Black Goddess," Kate Rushin

"All of us hunt identity."
—"Black Studies, June Jordan"

in the dark, candlelit room you try not to appear
as the woman at her wits end, wringing a cloth soaked
in tears. you try not to look like you are pleading
though you sit on a stool, just a few inches off the ground,
meaning you have to look up to meet his gaze, shadowed
by the brim of his hat. you try to control your voice
and hands from shaking—audibly, visibly. and
as far as you know, you are not this woman,
this image of hysterical distress, but you do know
that the only reason you've landed here,
in the back room of a hoodoo shop in new orleans,
conferring with a houngan is because, you say,
you don't know what to do next. or, more accurately,
you wonder to yourself, half mockingly, half earnest,
how many ways are there to name a wound?
what verbiage could pacify the flutter in your chest
i thought that merely pointing to the thing would make it shrivel
inward, scabbing over to leave nothing but a silk pink memory.

a blink turned to dust and no wonder

afraid I am not afraid I am not afraid I
am not afraid I am not afraid I am not afraid I am not afraid I am not afraid I

i tried telling all of my secrets

to a cactus in the desert

its flower opening in the moonlight

afraid I a

for three straight days

i was not thirsty i did not speak

i bled in the sand & here again a stone appeared

a glittering red garnet

a fist clenching

the motherwound

a deep sound resonating

The seventh episode of *Lovecraft Country's* premiere season, titled "I am." is the only title that includes punctuation. Period. This episode follows Hippolyta (Aunjanue Ellis), the matriarch of the Freeman family who, until this point, was largely ignored or pushed aside even though it is clear that she is equally if not more intelligent, capable, and observant than her husband George (Courtney B. Vance) who researches and authors the *Safe Negro Travel Guide*, reminiscent of *The Negro Motorist Greenbook* by Victor Hugo Green, in that they are both intended to give Black Americans a map to navigate a racist country, to provide safe passage. Hippolyta often wishes to accompany him on these trips, but he holds fast to the idea that it isn't safe and she remains at home with their daughter, Diane 'Dee' Freeman (Jada Harris). George, however, meets his demise in the second episode, "Whitey's on the Moon," having had an unfortunate brush with the magic of the Braithwaite family.

Upon returning from this trip, her nephew, Atticus 'Tic' Freeman (Jonathan Majors), and brother-in-law, Montrose Freeman (Michael Kenneth Williams), tell Hippolyta that he was killed at the hands of a police officer rather than trying to explain the possibility of the magic they witnessed which, prior to setting off on their mythic journey, none of them could have imagined. For five episodes, we see her on the periphery grieving and frustrated because she intuitively feels that the truth has been hidden from her. That this information is being withheld for her presumed safety is uniquely tied to the ways in which her identity, and thus self-determining power, has been stifled up to this point. Finally, having found the demolished Braithwaite mansion and one of Dee's comics that she often wrote for her father before he left for guide trips among the rubble, she becomes determined to take matters into her own hand.

in a cave
she descends
a wild persephone
teeth chattering in the hollow
of her skull

"In America, the traditional routes to Black identity have hardly been normal. Suicide (disappearance by imitation, or willed extinction), violence (hysterical religiosity, crime, armed revolt), and exemplary moral courage; none of these is normal.

And, if we consider humankind, if we consider the origins of human society, we realize that, in America, the traditional routes to white identity have not been normal, either. Identity of a person has been pursued through the acquisition of material clues admittedly irrelevant to the achievement of happiness. Identity has been secured among water objects ceaselessly changing value. Worse, the marketplace has vanquished the workable concept of homeground or, as children say in their games, home-safe."

1

& looking for answers

The scene opens on Hippolyta surrounded by papers, drafting tools, notes with equations scrawled across them, and astronomical maps, in an attempt to decode Hiram's orrery, a golden replica of the solar system but with two suns. She knows it is encoded with the secrets that will lead her to solid ground, to clarity. After struggling with the shining lever-like arms of the contraption, and shifting her perspective, realizing that the planets needed to "tilt based on how they rotate on their axis," she clicks the correct pieces to place and the orrery comes to life revealing a key, the inscription "Every beginning is in time, and every limit of extension in space," and the coordinates 39.805499, -95.159492, the exact location of which is Mayfield, KS. She is quick to pack the car and get on the road.

she gets slow motion planet tilted and she can hear

the ether ringing
itching to tell

"Contemporary female autobiographers such as Lorde and Kingston blend the 'mythic' and 'realistic' modes in order to focus on the potential of the actualized self and to invoke a collective voice, emphasizing the cultural influences that enable or hinder this self-actualization."

2

of a time when wounds were mouths

"As rendered and racial subjects, black women speak/write in multiple voices - not all simultaneously or with equal weight, but with various and changing degrees of intensity, privileging one parole and then another. One discovers in these writers a kind of internal dialogue reflecting an intrasubjective engagement with the intersubjective aspects of self, a dialectic neither repressing difference nor, for that matter, privileging identity, but rather expressing engagement with the social aspects of self ('the other[s] in ourselves'). It is this subjective plurality (rather than the notion of the cohesive or fractured subject) that, finally, allows the black woman to become an expressive site for a dialectics/ dialogics of identity and difference."

3

the first step is always to point directly to the place that hurts

It is this multiplicity that I am after. It is this multiplicity that contains echoes of the hybrid as subject and object. It is akin to the "polyvocality" Evie Shockley references wherein she recognizes "the extent to which [a poem's] language, tone, diction, form, and other stylistic choices generate the effect of multiplicity in a single speaker's voice to create space for a number of different speakers—an effect that runs counter to (or around) the predominant expectation for lyric poems to function as internally consistent, first-person utterances." Polyvocality, to put it simply, can translate to organizational methods for activism that hinges on a simple premise—there is strength in numbers.

4

and the tilting magic spread like a lightness in the head
where she knows
always & already

"Biomythography melds nonfiction and myth, while placing a personal narrative amidst the many communities that person exists within. It challenges the lines between fiction and non-fiction while also questioning the singularity of autobiography."

5

we get stuck in our own loops and spirals

However, this departure doesn't come without resistance from both her daughter, Dee, and her nephew, Tic, and his co-adventurer and love interest, Letitia 'Leti' Lewis (Jurnee Smollett). The former is still grieving her father's death while the latter hope to continue their own quest for answers. Dee refuses to go through the departure rituals that she often did with her father and Leti and Tic just want to borrow the car that she's already packed and ready to leave in.

and all she can hear is no

At this point, nearly every character has been transformed by their interactions with magic except for Hippolyta who has been shielded from the truth of the unfolding fantasy world. Though she hasn't yet been initiated into this world, she is far from untouched by its effects and consequences.

through the thinning of the veil

As Hippolyta sets out in her 1984 Packard Station Sedan that the family lovingly calls "Woody," she sings along to Josephine Baker's "Piel Canela" with the windows down. The sun is shining, and she is out on the open road. Finally, she is affirmed in tasting the freedom she has always craved. The kind of freedom that the enslaved ancestor, Hanna, who intermittently appears to Leti and Tic in dreams with prophetic assistance, wishes for her descendants.

so i can't stay here knowing full well

"The sun is singing
    the sky is singing
        I am singing into the day
            moving
beyond
    all   boundaries."

6

i have every opportunity to leave

She sees a dark-skinned Black woman who has been identified as Bessie Stringfield, the first Black woman to motorcycle alone through all 48 connected states. She flaunts a green knuckle hat, a billowing white blouse, and matching white scarf that dances in the wind as she rides. The women exchange smiles existing in one another's orbit for just a moment.

are you sure sweetheart that

you want to be well

somewhere there was sky to suit here sand to shape her and ocean to savor

"The 'oneness of being' is predicated on Man being an *integrated* and *indispensable* part of the universe. Being-in-the-world also means to participate in its social time. Hence, to be is to be what you are because of your historical part as well as what you anticipate to be your historical future. In recognizing the historical grounding of one's being, one has also to accept the collective and social sense of one's history. In taking as one's own the collective and social history of one's people, one in turn, realizes that his 'self' is not contained only in his physical presence in finite time. The twin notions of *interdependence* and *oneness of being* allows for a conception of self which transcends, through the historical consciousness of one's people, the finiteness of both Newtonian space and time.

Self-awareness is not therefore limited to just the cognitive awareness of one's uniqueness, individuality and historical finiteness (as in the Euro-American tradition). It is the awareness of self as an awareness of one's historical consciousness (collective spirituality) and the sense of 'we' being one."

i was unmoored

in an unraveling prayer

7

curling like smoke in afternoon light

As Hippolyta drives, she finds the comic her daughter traditionally writes and illustrates for every guide trip in her lunch basket titled *The Interplanetary Adventures of Orinthya Blue*. More than perspective, this episode is about reflections. Not only is Hippolyta shown the many blueprints of black feminine existential possibility, but the viewers, Black women especially, are indulged in the same radical dreaming of the future.

nothing could guard me & yet space held

She arrives in Mayfield, KS at an observatory when it is dark and spots the full moon in the distance. That the sun has set only reinforces the fear perpetuated by the sun-down towns highlighted in episode one, "Sundown." Part of the horror element that is highlighted in the show is not just monsters and myths, but the reality of systems of oppression in 1950s America that the audience understands to have changed little to date.

in my absence

a rule of thumb

So, to understand the subject one must understand not just one's self but one's selves and how they interact intrapersonally and interpersonally. "The type of knowledge with which African Psychology is concerned is [...] more closely associated with an Eastern esoteric tradition which recognizes *self-knowledge* as the ultimate source of all knowledge."

8

an astral guide a map of scars

The challenge then is twofold: 1) articulating a name and then 2) giving the name a cosmology, a mythos, a story by which they are motivated to act. Counterstorytelling as a mode of survival becomes crucial here. Defined as "writing that aims to cast doubt on the validity of accepted premises or myths, especially ones held by the majority," counterstorytelling is most radical in Audre Lorde's *Zami: A Biomythography*.

9

The authors continue stating, "Society constructs the social world through a series of tacit agreements medicated by images, pictures, tales, tweets, blog postings, social media and other scripts. Much of what we believe is ridiculous, self-serving, or cruel but is not perceived to be so at the time. Attacking embedded preconceptions that marginalize others or conceal their humanity is a legitimate function of all fiction."

10

skinning the palms of my hands

knees hot with freshly peeled skin

this is how kneeling you make stone a part of you

"The Black personality which has ostensibly adjusted to Western Society is characterized by what Euro-American psychologists would call a 'schizoid' adjustment. This means that he lives in two worlds which diametrically differ on many key dimensions. He works to foster an image which will make him acceptable to the material world of the European (e.g., high achievement motivation, emphasis on cognition to the exclusion of affective experience and individualism.[ )] And on the other hand, he will attempt to maintain at least tenuous ties to his opposite Black origins."

At the observatory she finds a machine that matches the orrery and she quickly begins to work to decode it to understand its operation. "Mass, rotation, velocity, and radius" she repeats to herself. "The length of time it takes for each planet to travel around two suns." As she sits by the telescope frantically scribbling on her travel guide notes, equations appear encircling her in a glowing light. She returns to the machine and adjusts a few dials just as two officers enter the room. They notice the machine lit up and whirring and quickly stumble upon her hiding place. They begin questioning her aggressively as Tic appears on the scene just in time to assist. Leti, upon having found the orrery in Hippolyta's home where she was staying to help her sister Ruby (Wunmi Mosaku) babysit Dee, calls Tic to warn him that Hippolyta may be in trouble.

i fell into more open jaws than i can count

so i fed my wounds healing herbs & coconut water

The confrontation quickly turns into a scuffle as one officer draws his gun and both Tic and Hippolyta begin exchanging blows with each officer until Hippolyta is punched in the face, falling backward onto the machine causing it to go haywire. Meanwhile Tic disarms the officer he is fighting but both officers continue to attack him. As the machine begins to flash, smoke, and spin in the background, Hippolyta gets to her feet and, having found the officer's gun, takes aim. Suddenly, a portal appears behind the three men, warping and flashing, opening and closing on different landscapes: mountains, lakes, space, clouds. Tic throws the officer nearest him into the portal and Hippolyta pulls the trigger on the remaining officer, killing him. As Hippolyta moves to stand by Tic, he takes the gun from her and they hold hands, staring down on the officer's body with disbelief. Just then, Hippolyta is sucked into the portal and we fall with her into an amniotic spacescape.

"Self-preservation warned some of us that we could not afford to settle for one easy definition, one narrow individuation of self."

12

what would i name myself now that i could

"Jennifer Gillan notes the ways in which Zami follows a tradition of women's biographical writing and the ways in which biomythography often searches and writes into being a sense of home. In analyzing "journeywoman" narratives such as Zami and Gloria Anzaldúa's Borderlands / La Frontera: The New Mestiza, Gillan notices the similarities in form and content. She says that each of these biomythographies 'is part authobiography, poetry, revisionary history, and narrative which switches between locations and languages, often recalling Linda Lorde's [Audre Lorde's mother's] sensual language of home' (211). Thise theme of home, and more specifically searching for and naming home across place, is one way to understand how biomythography serves as a productive fragmentation of identity. Gillan goes on to say as '[a]n elongated poetic metaphor of what Caren Kaplan had called deterritorialized identity, the biomythography tells the story of a self constantly in the process of becoming, of a home which can be relocated at particular historical moments to meet particular needs' (211). Paule Marshall's Triangular Road continues this tradition. Biomythography is a way of renaming oneself, of self-actualization, of becoming human and legend in the telling of one's story (Weekes 2006). Audre Lorde becomes Zami. Valenza Pauline Burke becomes Paule Marshall. And each, in telling the specifics of their personal stories, places herself within a new history and a broader community.

Biomythography, as a form, illumines the multiple subjectivities of the subject, blurs the lines between individual and community, and provides the space for possibility, the space to reimagine the subject and her/his communities in alternative spaces, times, and from different perspectives. [...] Biomythography needs multiple narratives in order to be complete, and thus regardless of the status or social location of these supporting narratives, they become a necessary part of understanding the individual. The form of biomythography then, is how an individual narrative can find meaning in and through multiple lives, experiences, and perhaps most importantly, communities that have shaped the subject (Floyd-Thomas and Gillman 185)."

13

A galaxy explodes around her as she fallfloats, resembling the neural networks that you may remember seeing in science textbooks. It feels like the start of a creation myth. At one moment, she even curls into a fetal shape and appears to be a child in a womb. She picks up speed and appears to be a meteor hurtling toward a planet.

extraterrestrial waterbirth evidence that stranger though i get i am known inside myself

"The interior intersubjectivity is predicated, then, on *speaking*. If we cannot identify a 'first' step here in any systematic way, we can put our finger on the point: to overcome the officially imposed silence engendered by exclusive traditions of power—state- and corporate-sponsored—that, in turn, go on to be taken over by 'personality,' under the influence of those powers that properly belong to the repertoires of learning and naming that both 'piggyback' on the self-evidentiary wisdom of 'received opinion' (i.e., IQ, testing, bell curves, the criminality of the poor, etc.) and help to create it; in brief, the weight of the discursive debris that comes to rest on subjects a priori the local and specific fields of cultural play that they are called upon to negotiate. [...] Perhaps the speaking of intersubjectivity effects a kind of mimicry of the professional wordsmith's relationship to symbolic capital, but how is the speaking I mean hear to be differentiated from professional discourse?"

14

a liminal space of inner outer

A white architecturally amorphous building stands in front of her, seemingly the only building in an otherwise barren landscape. The building begins to glow brighter and two figures appear. It is unclear whether these are robots, humans, or otherworldly beings, but they walk towards her without hesitation.

a space that exists "beyond" what we know

Coordinates: 39.805499, -95.159492.265749

Coordinates appear frequently as she continues her interdimensional travel allowing for a kind of speculative fiction which, on the one hand, archives even the possibility of her existence in various times in space, but which also, on the other hand, reveals the very real ways in which Black women's healing is nonlinear, interdimensional even.

"A break toward the potentiality of becoming or the formation of substitutive identities, consists in going beyond what is given; it is also the exceeding of necessity." 15

Homi Bhaba calls this the "space for intervention." 16

Immediately after, the scene cuts to an all-white room and a new set of coordinates appear: 85.264793, 74.694721, 33.281947.

she tied paper to her wrists with rubber bands kissed ink

Hippolyta, who awakens from a seemingly unconscious state, lies naked on a black table, a gray jumpsuit folded at her feet. There is nothing else in the room though it is large, with its high, domed ceiling. As she sits up and looks around, she notices two "viewing windows" glowing purple on her wrists. Panicked and feeling trapped in an unknown place, she quickly gets to her feet, puts on the jumpsuit, and begins cautiously inspecting the space. Soon after, two doors slide open to reveal a woman, named Seraphina / Beyond C'est (Karen LeBlanc), a name that translates from Hebrew as "the purifying angel", that is two or three times Hippolyta's size and wearing the same futuristic gear that the two figures who found her had only, without the helmet, we see that this is a Black woman with an afro that is ten times the size of her face.

she absently slices her finger adding red

Hippolyta asks "Who are you? What are you?" and the woman replies "I am." Hippolyta continues, "Where am I? What are these things in my arms?" The woman stares at her in silence, unmoved and unaffected. Hippolyta, noticing that these questions didn't elicit an answer says, "You can't keep me here" and the woman replies "You are not in a prison" as she walks away, and the doors slide closed again. Hippolyta screams to be released, pounding on the door so hard that she breaks the glass and cuts herself, marking the door with her own blood. She falls into a sort of fugue state, and we may even understand that time becomes meaningless, having no discernable way to mark its passage or escape. She rips at the things in her wrists and soon after tears the sleeves from her jumpsuit to cover / hide her wrists. Another set of coordinates appears across the screen: 85.264793, 74.694721, 34.971465.

you whisper to yourself

articulate with language

i believed the space-time continuum

"In this sense, 'overcoming' is the cancellation of what is given. Borch-Jacobsen offers this explanation: 'Thus language, the manifestation of the negativity of the subject who posits himself by negating (himself as) the Real, works the miracle of manifesting what is not; the tearing apart, the ek-sistence, and the perpetual self-overtaking that 'is' the subject who speaks himself in everything by negating everything.' 'speaking' here is both process and paradigm, to the extent that signifying enables the presence of an absence and registers the absence of a presence, but it is also a superior mark of the transformative, insofar as it makes something by cutting through the 'pure and simple' of the 'undifferentiated' in the gaps and spacings of signifiers. If potentiality, then, can be said to be the site of the human, rather than the nonhuman fixedness—more precisely, if it is the 'place' of the subjectivity, the condition of being/becoming subject—then its mission is to unfold through 'words, words, words,' yes, but 'words, words, words' as they lead us out of the re-presentational where the subject commences its journey in the looking glass of the symbolic.

Thus, to represent a self through masks of self-negation is to take on the work of discovering where one 'is at'—the subject led back to his signifying dependence. [...] We could speak of this process as the subject making its mark through the transitivity of reobjectivations, the silent traces of desire on which the object of the subject hinges."

17

couldn't hold as much of me as i was able to accept

She begins to make observations about her environment: "Salt in the air on the beach. Sufficient oxygen. I didn't get dizzy when I wasn't on the ship. Is it a ship? Am I on another planet? The sand was strangely springy." Another set of coordinates: 85.264793, 74.694721, 35.842368. "No, I was to arrive at the root lighter. Not like Orithya Blue on Mars, but just enough to feel it in my tendons. Gravity turned down just a notch." She paces the room, smacks her head wracking for answers, solutions, knowledge, a way to describe and define what she was experiencing. warm as a heartbeat

love ain't flesh and muscle like it could be

one of salt

speak life into

the honey

"What would Dad say?" Coordinates: 85.264793, 74.694721, 37.149785. "Gustav Mie. He warned of gravity shifts in the future. There's no known planet with sustainability. Was she human?" Finally, she begins examining the table from which she arose, the only other thing in the room and begins to disassemble the table. Coordinates: 85.264793, 74.694721, 41.942574. "64 number settings. Froom 000 to 999." When she lets go of each puzzle-like piece of the table it defies gravity. "Makes the total possible combinations ten to the 192nd power. 63 trillion celestial panoramas." Her mental state moves from entrapment, to observation, to awe. Once she stops resisting, once she lets go of the narrative of being trapped, she begins to see her other options.

With a piece of the table that she broke off she is able to peel back one of the panels in the room to reveal writes that she begins to unscrew. This prompts the return of Seraphina who repels Hippolyta backward just by raising her hand. Hippolyta charges her and is again restrained by the invisible force Seraphina wields. Hippolyta screams "Let me go" and the woman responds once again with "you are not in a prison. Where do you want to be?" "Name yourself" she repeats, and Hippolyta burst out into laughter "What the fuck are you talking about?" The woman says again "Where do you want to be? Name it. Who do you want to be? Name it. Name it." Hippolyta says, exasperated, "I want to be dancing on stage in Paris with Josephine Baker."

imagine the remedy that ends the split

"[I]n West African naming systems, the question of naming is a vital one…throughout your life, in Yoruba traditions, when something important happens, you gain another name, or you are given another name. […] So the process of naming is a process of rebirth. And it is something that is happening in the book. Now, Zami is a word that is used in Carriacou, meaning women who work and live together, and it is a very beautiful word. […] I didn't know what it meant, I didn't know that it meant women-identified women, women who love each other, but when I came across it, I really wanted to claim it as my own, as a Black lesbian. And, originally, it probably came from Patois, which is a combination of French and Spanish, probably from 'les amies,' the friends. (qtd. in Kraft 149)." 18

unlearning an echo halfway between thresholds

"sing her song of life
she's been dead so long
closed in silence so long
she doesn't know the sound
of her own voice
her infinite beauty
she's half-notes scattered
without rhythms/ no tune
sing her sighs
sing the song of her possibilities
sing a righteous gospel
let her be born
let her be born
& handled warmly." 19

i was interrupted but

made of the answers

i feel my voice start to change blooming

space and time like a kaleidoscope

aren't i holy aren't we

proof enough

Immediately we are transported to 1920s Paris. Coordinates: 52.263231, -49.988712, 65.941543. Hippolyta, who up until now had worn modest clothing befit for a 1950s housewife, now wears a white feather headdress with matching feather bra, diamond earrings and a diamond choker, silver spanks, a negligée-like skirt that is also lined with feathers, and silver pumps. She stumbles through the choreography hardly able to believe where she is. The dance number ends with all the dancers topless. As the dancers berate her for ruining the number, even going so far as to hurl "go back where you came from," Baker approaches Hippolyta as a mentor to take her under her wing. Baker shows her the steps and retreats to her dressing room. Coordinates: 52.263231, -49.988712, 67.429781.

It's unclear the exact amount of time that Hippolyta spends in this time and space, but it is long enough to learn the choreography, become close friends with Baker and someone who notices when she has "that look again", and explores what is being framed as queerness. Frida Khalo (Camila Canó-Flaviá) makes a toast "Here's to the girls like us who know when to create, and when to destroy."

Josephine: "Me, I feel like the stars in the black of space—magnificent, ancient, and already extinguished."

"A psychoanalytic culture criticism would not only attempt to name such contradictions but would establish the name of inquiry itself as the goal of an *interior subjectivity*. As it seems clear to me at the moment, the African-American collective denotes the quintessential object of the discourses of social science, insofar as the overwhelming number of commentaries concerning it have to do with the 'findings' of the sociological and the collective situation within the economy. The limitation of this view, if not of particular projects, is that it achieves little perspective with a 'general science of the economy of practices.' What is more, naming here becomes destiny, to the extent that the social formation, or individual communities within it, more accurately, comprehend themselves, almost entirely, as an innocence or a passivity worked upon, worked over, by others. While it would be much too simplistic and erroneous to say, 'all we have to doo…' we can guess without apology that there is an aspect of human agency that cannot be bestowed or restored by others, even though the philosopher's 'recognition,' or lack of it, will, in fact, support it, and it is this aspect of the historical and cultural apprenticeship—strategies for gaining agency—that we wish to describe in a systematic way.

I have chosen to call this strategy the *interior subjectivity*, which I would, in turn, designate as the locus at which *self-interrogation* takes place. It is not an arrival but a departure, not a goal but a process, and it conduces to neither an answer nor a 'cure,' because it is not engendered in formulae and prescriptions. More precisely, its operations are torque-like to the extent that they throw certainty an dogma (the static, passive, monumental aim) into doubt. This process situations a content to work on as a discipline, as an askesis, and I would specify it on the interior because it is found in economy but is not exhausted by it. Persistently motivated in inwardness, in-flux, it is the 'mine' of social production that arises, I part, from interacting with others, yet it bears the imprint of a particularity. In the rotations of certainty, this 'mine' gets away with very little, scot-free, and *that*, I believe, rebounds back upon the ethical wish that commences this writing.

[…] In the wake of loss, we only have left, it seems, the inexorable grimness of 'competition,' of 'getting over,' of role-model-ing,' of 'success' for the well-credentialed, and a thorough commodification of black culture." **20**

if you can name yourself

Hippolyta: "Now that I'm tasting it, freedom, like I've never known before, I see what I was robbed of back then. All those years I thought I had everything I ever wanted, only to come here and discover that all I ever was was the exact kind of Negro woman white folks wanted me to be. I feel like they just found a smart way to lynch me without me noticing the noose. […] I hate me, hate me, for letting them make me feel small. And I hate…" she trails off and Baker comes in. "Who else do you hate? So, Miss Hippolyta, what are you going to do with all that anger?" Hippolyta then repeats three times, crescendo-ing into a near-scream "I am Hippolyta."

The fact that she must scream, exalt in her own name as ecstatic release and near-cry signifies the restrictions from which she releases herself. She becomes limitless.

She is transported to another time and space. Coordinates: -25.164754, 52.021799, 12.365684.

until the whole thing begins again

A small village appears as she stands in the center of a small circle of female warriors in training. "All that screaming won't save you now. You're not making a baby you're in a fucking fight" her new mentor, Nawi (Sufe Bradshaw), spits at her. She begins to make a speech about the necessity for fighting saying: "I will tell you why you are here and why you must get up. You are here because you did not believe them. Your whole life, they told you you were free, and when they said that, they meant you were free to cook their food, free to raise children, their children, free to work for them. They even lied to you and told you you were free to run the world. But it is still their world. You are here because you knew that all they offer that a well-kept slave could ever ask for. Now, I cannot tell you what true freedom is. You have got to find that for yourself. But today you are still too afraid to go looking."

i am whole

i am love and love and love

i am perfect and right and divine

in all my totality

Coordinates: -25.164754, 52.021799, 14.742656
-25.164754, 52.021799, 17.945463
-25.164754, 52.021799, 20.347881
-25.164754, 52.021799, 22.941242
-25.164754, 52.021799, 25.469562
-25.164754, 52.021799, 26.469562
-25.164754, 52.021799, 29. 754812

A training sequence ensues as we see Hippolyta in a new definition of who she can be. Not just demure, sexy, and riffing to jazz but a warrior who has no other option but to fight. Similar to her Josephine Baker outfit, she is adorned in cowrie shells where once she was dripping in diamonds. Again, there is no clear indicator of time other than the quickening progression of coordinates that flash across the screen and we see Hippolyta rise in the ranks to become the leader of her unit.

the spell she is spinning around herself

Coordinates: -25.164754, 52.021799, 35.518776.

Hippolyta goes into battle against what appears to be confederate soldiers. Covered in blood, and wearing all gold including her newly gifted golden helmet with a long tale of feathers that flows over her shoulders and down her back, Hippolyta fights with a kind of fierceness we have seen hints of in her anger and grief over her husband, now fully realized as a useful tool.

Hippolyta: "We are here because we did not believe them when they told us our rage was not ladylike. We did not believe them when they said our violence goes too far. We did not believe them when they said that the hatred that we feel for our enemies is not godlike. They say that to women like us because they know what happens when we are free, free to hate when we must, free to kill when we must, free to bring destruction when we must. That is our freedom, that is our prayer no matter what they think of us after we grind them into the dust. That is our love." She raises her sword and her fellow warriors cheer. Then, she drops her sword, removes her helmet, knowing that defeat is at her back, and says, "I am Hippolyta. George's wife."

someone told me that you deal in wormholes or that i can only follow you so far down

This second declaration of her self-hood is quieter, more of an acceptance of her new reality than an inflamed anger for the reality from which she came.

like warping portals to the version of myself i have not yet imagined

Once again, the scene dissolves and she reappears in bed, next to her husband, one of the first scenes that introduces us to these characters recalled from episode one.

i remember i mistook an ambulance siren

Coordinates: 88.649896, -78.226541, 98.659971.

for a wild woman laughing

Though the scene begins the same as when we first saw it, the difference now is that Hippolyta tells George about everything she's seen and experienced.

"It wasn't another planet at all, and it wasn't a time machine. […] That's when I knew that the equation in the many worlds theory had to be accurate. […] Baby, a world where I can name myself anything."

George asks if what they are experiencing is real and she isn't sure but says it feels real.

"You still named yourself my wife," George says, quietly astounded.

and the whole world folded side-stitched

"the truth is
my life has slipped out
of my possession." 21

"I think now I can name this thing that's been eating at me quietly, so quiet. Sometimes, I thought I was tired, sad, or missing you when you were out on the road but really, I was angry. So angry because for so much of my life, I've been shrinking. When I was a kid, I thought I was big enough to have every right to name something out of this world, and then I just started shrinking myself. By the time I met you I had already gotten so small and I thought you knew how big I wanted to be. I thought you saw me. But you just stood by and let me shrink myself more for you."

from the cure the smile carved

in the universe

"my love is too beautiful to have thrown back on my face." 22

We recall that in episode four, "A History of Violence," when accompanies Tic, Leti, and Montrose to a museum in Boston so she can take Dee to the planetarium she reveals, as they lie on their backs gazing at the ceiling, that when she was young she entered a contest to name a comet. She called it "Hera's Chariot" and had won the contest, but credit was attributed to the niece of an astronomer in Sweden named Nancy Studabaker. "The astronomical society who held the naming contest didn't want a little colored girl to be the face of their competition," Hippolyta says. "You should've fought that, Mama." She replies, "We know the truth." Upon learning this Dee exclaims, "Y'all see that comet. My mama named it! My momma named Hera's Chariot. Now they know the truth too." It is an episode that highlights colonial and imperialist "discovery" notably that of Braitwaite's himself. A tour guide says: "In this, one of our museum's oldest sections, we see the many artifacts the famed explorer Titus Braitwaite was given in exchange for teaching the savage tribes the ways of civilized man." A very *Black Panther* moment a la Killmonger in the Museum of Great Britain.

they say the sun is

the dark divine

what it means to know and speak

the end of a cycle

self-fulfilling prophecy

"Our women
the ones left behind
always know the taste
of their own strength—
bitter at times it might
be." 23

Hippolyta often experienced the limitations imposed upon her by nearly everyone around her, including her husband, loving as he may have been. So, when she is finally able to articulate what has been gnawing at her, George stumbles, asks why she didn't say something sooner, makes excuses and then, finally, pauses to say, "You're right." He recognizes the ways in which he was complicit in keeping her small for his own benefit and apologizes. She gets her flowers while she is still living. "I see you now, Hippolyta Freeman," he says, "And I want you to be as big as you can be."

who told you your dreams were not good enough to sit on

She replies, "I am Hippolyta. Discoverer." She extends her hand to him and as he takes it, their hands encircled by the magic embedded in her wrists, purple glitter, and the scene dissolves again.

Coordinates: 48.377481, 99.549847, 36.632478.

my body wanted only future   only you

They are on another planet in a spaceship that resembles their earthly vehicle, Woody. She now resembles Orithya Blue and is an explorer in her own right. Eventually, she returns to Seraphina saying, "I got curious."

"For the first time in my life, I had an insight into what poetry could be. I could use words to recreate that feeling, rather than to create a dream, which was what so much of my writing had been before." 24

the time you asked her what she wanted and she said it   more

"i found god in myself
& i loved her fiercely." 25

Seraphina: "Now that you've named yourself, we can fully integrate you into our society."

Hippolyta: "How can I fit everything that I am now into that place?"

The concept of home is located within the deepest recesses of the body. Most believe this is where the shadows of our selves hide, the things we want to be kept secret and unseen lodged between ligaments and awaiting an opportune moment to slip out. Upon returning to her family home Alice Walker talks with her mother about what it is she's hoping to find. The dialogue goes: "You look whole enough to me," she says. "No," I answer, "because everything around me is split up, deliberately split up. History split up, literature split up, and people are split up too. It makes people do ignorant things." 25

Because integration into this new world would mean leaving her daughter behind, Hippolyta understands that she must return home.

"I had never felt visible before, nor even known I lacked it." 27

The first step is always to point directly to the place that hurts.

she was prism reborn   she was sharp refracted everything*

"Armed with scars
healed
in many different colors
I look in my own faces
as Eshu's daughter crying
if we do not stop killing
the other
in ourselves
the self that we hate
in others
soon we shall all lie
in the same direction." 28

"I am" statements and the excavational work that is required to unearth them are an exercise in mapping, of finding one's way back to the core, that most fundamental of foundations. Which is to say of naming your most essential parts so that you might replicate into a billion different possibilities.

Voiceover: [Sun Ra's *Space is the Place*] – "I'm not real. I'm just a reality; I come to you as the myth, because that's what Black

like you. [...] I do not come to you as people are. Myths."

i am the deepest spell spoken

she whispered to make her mouth her own*

Bambara, Toni Cade. *The Salt Eaters*. Vintage, 1992.

5, 13 — Bascomb, Lia T. "Water, Roads, and Mapping Diaspora Through Biomythography." *Anthurium: A Caribbean Studies Journal*. Vol. 14.1, 2017, Article 10.

16 — Bhaba, Homi. *The Location of Culture*. 2nd ed. Routledge, 1994.

7, 8, 11 — Clark, Cedric X. et al. "Voodoo or IQ: An Introduction to African Psychology." *Journal of Black Psychology*, Vol. 1.2, Feb. 1975, pp. 9-29.

9, 10 — Delgado, Richard and Jean Stefanic. *Critical Race Theory: An Introduction*, 3rd. ed. New York UP, 2017.

Gumbs, Alexis Pauline. *Spill: Scenes of Black Feminist Fugitivity*. Duke UP, 2016.

3 — Henderson, Mae G. "Speaking in Tongues: Dialogics, Dialectics, and the Black Woman Writer's Literary Tradition." *African American Literary Theory*. Winston Napier, ed. New York UP, 2000, pp. 348-368.

"I am." *Lovecraft Country*, created by Misha Greene, performances by Aunjanue Ellis, Jurnee Smollett, and Jonathan Majors, season 1, episode 7, Bad Robot, Monkeypaw Productions, and Warner Bros. Television, 2019.

1 — Jordan, June. "Black Studies: Bringing Back the Person." *Civil Wars*. Beacon Press, 1981, pp. 45-55.

12, 24, 27 — Lorde, Audre. *Zami: A New Spelling of My Name*. 2nd ed. Crossing Press, 2001.

28 — Lorde, Audre. "Between Ourselves." *The Collected Poems of Audre Lorde*. Norton, 1997, pp. 223.

6, 21, 23 — Nichols, Grace. *I Is a Long Memoried Woman*. Karnak House, 1983.

19, 22, 25 — Shange, Ntozake. *For Colored Girls Who Have Considered Suicide When the Rainbow Is Enuf*. Scribner, 1997.

4 — Shockley, Evie. "Introduction: Renegade Poetics (Or, Would Black Aesthetics by An[y] Other Name Be More Innovative?). *Renegade Poetics: Black Aesthetics and Formal Innovation in African American Poetry*. Iowa UP, 2011, pp. 1-24.

14, 15, 17, 20 — Spillers, Hortense. "'All the Things You Could Be By Now, If Sigmund Freud's Wife Was Your Mother': Psychoanalysis and Race." *Black, White, and in Color*. Chicago UP, 2003, pp. 376-427.

26 — Walker, Alice. "In Search of Our Mothers' Gardens." *In Search of Our Mothers' Gardens*. Harcourt, 1983, pp. 231-243.

2, 18 — Weekes, Karen. "Othered Writers, Other Forms: Biomythography and Automythography." *Genre* XXXIX, Summer 2006, pp. 329-346.

& the portal appears

DESTINY HEMPHILL

(before proceeding, an invocation to be read aloud)

scarlet sky / fissured earth / cotton-mouthed / your hands clasped / across your splitting belly / in your craw / is the historical entanglement / the half-millennium long / planetary ecocide-genocide knot / known as "since 1492" / you were born into it / & it into you / churning, burning, bulging / within you / your ears ring / soften your craggy breath / now a hum / soften your craggy breath / now a song / now a song? / yes, a cicada song / burrowing into your skull / *go to the edge / not the bleached pit of the center / but the edge /* the song says / *go to the edge / no, not the hemorrhaged / mottling borders of empire. but beyond / elsewhere / go to the edge /* look down / slivers of moonrind so thin / they look like / they could slice / the souls of your feet / illumine your path / you follow them / sometimes you walk, slither, hop / along the slivers of moonrind / to the edge / sometimes the knot makes it that you are writhing / convulsing / revolting / to the edge / to the edge, nonetheless / the edge be a liminal space / & you know liminal ≠ marginal / (& if you don't know, now you know) / but rather, liminal be a ritual / space / & a ritual space be for summoning / & transformation / when you arrive / the fragrance / of mulberry trees / washes over you / it is dusk / you are not alone here / others surround you with red threads / hanging from their mouths / you feel the knot / entangled within you / unravel / you all kneel / sink into the edge / pull the threads / from each of your own mouths / not always gently / not always gingerly / as you pull, unravel, disentangle / you swoon & sway in somnolence / a summoning hum then howl / comes from your throats / & as you summon other worlds, may other worlds summon you & as you summon another world, may another world summon you & as you summon mother-world, may motherworld summon   summon   summon

LANGUAGES OF LIBERATION, DISRUPTION, AND MAGIC

Text of Bliss: Heaping Disruption at the Level of Language

KENJI C. LIU

zuihitsu[1]

Today I received a Buddhist name: Yōshin, or "to embrace/protect heartmind." To find an appropriate name, the guideline was: It should be challenging. A customized aspiration.

Between now and the aspirational future, one certainty: a series of changes. A trajectory of breakages. I will write my way from here to there, or not.

*

"Text of pleasure: The text that contents, fills, grants euphoria; the text that comes from culture and does not break with it, is linked to a comfortable practice of reading.

Text of bliss: The text that imposes a state of loss, the text that discomforts (perhaps to the point of a certain boredom), unsettles the reader's historical, cultural, psychological assumptions, the consistency of [their] tastes, values,

---

[1] A form of Japanese literature made of loosely structured fragments, observations, ideas, essays that respond to the author's surroundings.

memories, brings to a crisis [their] relation with language." (Roland Barthes, *The Pleasure of the Text*, 14)

*

It seems as if it might rain. Where I grew up in New Jersey, rain usually announced its pending arrival; it sent humidity first, ominous clouds and wind. There are at least fifty words for rain in Japanese, but I can't find an exact match for wet air with a storm on its tail. Maybe 雨催い, amamoyoi, the threat of rain.

*

There is a place and time for the poetry of comfort and contentment, the poem that pleases aesthetically even if the subject is difficult. Beyond that, I think my poetry goal is to break something. Not in the sense of something broken in my interior, a confession and healing, but instead a methodical attempt to

break certain aspects of

this world.

*

... to bring to a crisis [their] relation with language.

*

Was there a time when my relationship with language was not fraught?

*

My parents would ask me to edit the English grammar and spelling of their business correspondences. As a child, I was endowed with the power of language and the language of power. I could ease our family's way by manipulating English.

After a while, I included imperfections. Experimentation with perception, authenticity, rank, expectation. Were these my first poems?

*

Native plants of Middlesex County, New Jersey: threeseed mercury, box elder, red maple, silver maple, sugar maple, calamus, white baneberry, black baneberry, northern maidenhair, false foxglove, yellow giant hyssop, white snakeroot, agrimony, bent grass, white colicroot, water plantain, …

*

Kotodama (言霊, word spirit), the Shinto belief in the mystical power of words and names. Word and thing, inseparable. A word does not call to a thing, it is the thing itself.

言 = word = koto
事 = thing = koto

If sign and signifier are not a relationship but a single thing, then to use a word is to actually conjure and activate what it refers to. To write poetry is to cast a spell.

Editing a parent's letter might impact a matter way beyond the child's comprehension … is this magic?

*

Magic, possibly from *magh-

Proto-Indo-European root meaning "to be able," "to have power."

*

As a child, I was disappointed to find that magic classes were really about how to create the illusion of magic. Simple or elaborate, everything was a trick. Magic words and phrases did not have any power, they were just trimmings for the main event of trickery. I don't like to be tricked. How short my magic career was.

*

"Just as was the case with modern magic, [Western] magicians were deeply conflicted about the meaning and integrity of Oriental magic— they were torn between wanting to believe in a distant but still-living space of phantasmagoria and also wanting to assert the developmental superiority and universal consistency of Western modernity. … For some, the idea of Oriental magic became a kind of flourish, like pixie dust, that could be cast over performances in London, Paris, and New York to help audiences find that precious feeling of Enchantment. Orientalism became a kind of magic in itself." (Chris Goto-Jones, *Conjuring Asia*, 5)

*

"All [magical] ritual is a kind of language, it therefore translates ideas." (Marcel Mauss, *A General Theory of Magic*, 75)

*

Performance magic, a performance of, a translation of … modernity, imperialism. A transaction?

*

手品 (tejina) refers to the illusion-based, sleight-of-hand type of magic. It very plainly uses the characters for "hand" (手) and "goods" (品) which basically amounts to someone's hand playing the cup and ball trick.

魔法 (mahou) refers to witchcraft, sorcery, spellcasting. 魔 (ma) is a witch, demon, or evil spirit, whereas 法 (hou) is method, law, or rule. Demon law. Witch method. Evil spirit rule.

*

In sympathetic magic, you bracket a piece of the larger target, work your spell on the isolate. Because the essence of the whole is also in the part, anything you do to one happens to the other.

*

… deconstruction, erasure, randomization, bibliomancy …

*

To transform a text into poetry through erasure—to break it. Especially when the text has a social sacredness.

When Tracy K. Smith erases the Declaration of Independence, she finds commentary about the slave trade inside a founding US national document. Relying on words already in the text, she finds slavery living in it ... the document indicts itself.

We have reminded them of the circumstances of our emigration
and settlement here.
      —taken Captive
                          on the high Seas

to bear—

*

"Each of us is here now because in one way or another we share a commitment to language and to the power of language, and to the reclaiming of that language which has been made to work against us." (Audre Lorde, "The Transformation of Silence into Language and Action," 41)

*

When very young, I was critiqued by a teacher for using too many commas in English sentences. Looking back, I wonder if this use of commas was related to my first language, Japanese, which is thick with pauses and silences. Unspoken meaning. A Japanese sentence can leave out the object, relying on context and relationship to fill in meaning, or it can be vague on purpose ... ...

... sometimes, without thinking, English comes from me ... structured by my first language, re/unstructured by Japanese. It is—

*

Think of silence as a violence, when silence means being made a frozen sea. Think of speaking as a violence, when speaking is a house that dresses your life in the tidiest wallpaper. (Chen Chen, "Kafka's Axe & Michael's Vest")

*

Things that are better once broken:

    eggs, cracked and cooked
    clouds, after long days of gloom
    world record for most dogs in a conga line (8)
    the English language

*

It's raining now. A light rain, 小雨. In David Lynch's version of *Dune,* the messiah Paul Atreides summons rain just by standing there and gazing into the air. I don't have a source for Spice, and neither do I have blue eyes.

*

I am a stranger to English, I am a stranger inside English. It was not meant for me, but I break it through my residence. Legislatures and courts have ruled against my residence many times, by defining citizenship against me and others. A legal maneuver, a language that casts a spell of borders, that protects the property of white supremacy. What is legal and illegal has no substance, it changes, it brackets, attempts to make a word into a thing. Nationalist kotodama magic.

*

The coziness of being driven around in the rain. In Los Angeles, people get freaked out by it and weave erratically.

*

"[Electronic Disturbance Theater] 1.0/2.0 has always been invested in experimental poetry as part of its gestures—from the found poetry of the '404 file not found' of our [Electronic Civil Disobedience] performances in [the] 1990s to the border hack actions with the Zapatista Tribal Port Scan in 2000 on US Border Patrol servers, where we would scan and upload Zapatista poems that we had written into their servers." (Ricardo Dominguez in *Media Fields Journal,* December 29, 2016)

*

To *cast*: from Old Norse kasta, to pile, throw, heap.

The *Oxford English Dictionary* lists sixty-nine outdated and contemporary meanings for cast.

> Spells must be correctly cast, pronounced …

*

> "We sleep in language, if language does not come to wake us with its strangeness." (Robert Kelly, "On Translation," 545)

For a long time I was asleep in English. For decades my dreams were monolingual.

*

… the Sapir-Whorf hypothesis … that language influences thought and perception? What if the original language is overlaid by a new one, but the former sometimes structures the latter?

*

I have been translating Japanese-language poetry written by issei, first-generation immigrants who came to the US between the world wars, an intensely anti-Asian period. In 1928 Los Angeles, Morio Hayashida writes:

> Autumn night's shadow
> A momentary meditation
> alone
> Following a foreign land's noise, the absent-minded immigrant gets
> sunburned
> Hungry for love
> Looking at the graveyard
> Fabricating a phantom homeland
> ("Cemetery," *Where to Go*)

Each image directs the reader to a variety of possible meanings in a way that transforms it. … a spacious invocation—cemetery in autumn, the dark growing longer. what shadow … of night? a hint of ominous? a moment of contemplation … line break … alone, a word by itself, the poet alone? alone and following a strange land's call, the immigrant … alone? absent-mindedly listening … noise, hypnotic, promising … what? … sunburned … again alone. Lonely, hungry … lonely. In the graveyard, a city of ghosts, a home? … where? in autumn's night shadow, in the cemetery?

*

Native plants of Los Angeles: Sand verbena, big leaf maple, box elder, red-skinned onion, red shanks, maidenhair fern, mountain dandelion, bent grass, white alder, beach-bur, western ragweed, false indigo bush, yerba mansa, …

*

"The poem's significance, both as a principle of unity and as the agent of semantic indirection, is produced by the *detour* the text makes as it runs the gauntlet of mimesis, moving from representation to representation, with the aim of exhausting the paradigm of all possible variations on the matrix." (Michael Riffaterre, *Semiotics of Poetry*, 19)

*

A poem is its own world with an internal set of rules. A poem is its own complete matrix of evolving, self-referential meaning. Every word is haunted by its past and potential variations.

A poem is a strangeness that arrives from—

*

… the etymology of *poetry* in English and Japanese—go back far enough, there are connections to oral traditions—through song or recitation. The distinctions between song, poem, prayer, and magic spell disappear.

*

I grew up in a home full of books, dusty-scented hardcovers of Japanese and Chinese arts and culture. It must have been in one of these where I first saw the thirteenth-century statue of Kūya, the Japanese Buddhist monk from three centuries before.

Kūya is reciting the six sounds of the nembutsu mantra (na mu a mi da butsu), each represented by a tiny figure of Amida Buddha streaming from his mouth, attached by a wire. Innovative and surreal, even by today's standards.

For Kūya, chanting the nembutsu worked miracles.

*

Kotodama:

"Souls reside within the words of Japan, and it will be filled with good luck due to the power they contain" (Kakinomoto no Hitomaro 3254, *Manyōshū [Collection of 10,000 Leaves]*, circa 759 CE)

*

A nationalist move, to associate language = spiritual power = nation. What if you go against the words? The invention of illegality.

*

Classical Japanese poetry is 歌 (uta), which also means song. The origin story of haiku: it used to be the entryway to longer oral poems, the tanka. The oldest recorded tanka are songs.

*

In the *Manyōshū*, there are approximately 160 plants mentioned in 1,500 poems, mostly tanka. Manyō shokubutsu-en are gardens planted specifically with these flora (similar to a Shakespeare garden)—poems embodied in land-scape, words and things together. A garden of Japan's mythical poetic origin. A garden of kotodama.

*

Plants in the *Manyōshū*: madder, matsutake, hemp, bellflower, fringed water lily, common reed, ashitsukinori, lily-of-the-valley bush, lacecap hydrangea, neem tree, curly mallow, bitter orange, sweet sedge, field mustard, …

*

One of the Japanese words for magic spell (呪文) contains the character jyu (呪 or 咒), consisting of two mouths and a pair of legs. If I look at these as visual poetry, perhaps the spell caster and the recipient. Or maybe the doubling of a single person's voice. The other character (文) is mon, which means sentence.

*

... old Buddhist traditions of magic casting that combine mantras with ritualistic, symbolic actions whose intention is a specific result—for example, that lightning strikes someone, or to gain heightened senses ...

*

In the original Chinese, the 魔 (ma) from 魔法 (mahou, spellcasting) is a mutation of the Sanskrit māra. Māra is the evil demon who tries to tempt and distract the Buddha the night he achieves complete enlightenment.

... a spell as distraction?

*

If poetry is song, is also spell, what does it open?

*

"The texts gathered here ... I would like them to be received as writing of the vertigo where book opens to book." (Edmond Jabès, *The Book of Margins*, 20)

Where writing opens to writing, poem opens to poem, sign-signifier-sign, the only way meaning comes to be known ... the book is unstable, it does not congeal. To write a new poem necessitates burrowing into multiple texts, multiple 魔rgins, and these texts write the new poem.

*

What heap, what accumulation of language has spelled the world we live in? What narrative vertigo must we write in order to destroy our world's languages of dominance and death?

*

. . . something here about passive language which can falsely erase power relations, erase who did what to who, its violence . . .

*

The Transborder Immigrant Tool (TBT) was an experimental Electronic Disturbance Theater/b.a.n.g. lab mobile phone "geo-poetic-system" (gps) designed to guide migrants crossing the Southern border to water caches, while also offering ecological poetry as emotional and mental sustenance during the deadly journey. Right-wing pundit Glenn Beck attacked the project, fearing a poetry that would "dissolve" the US's borders.

*

Native plants that dissolve the US-Mexico border: California buckwheat, desert broom, deerweed, chalk dudleya, alkali heliotrope, smallseed sandmat, barrel cactus, wishbone bush, arrowweed, cottonwood, fourwing saltbush, common sagebrush, coastal goldenbush, California boxthorn, white horehound, salt grass, . . .

*

When my grandmother visited me from Japan, I drove her to see the open, flat spaces of California . . . wide and dry . . .

*

Activism, when delivered through a "performance matrix" or "minor simulation," exists in a gray area:

> "The question of aesthetics, at least for us, creates a disturbance in the 'Law' to the degree that it cannot easily contain the 'break' and it is forced to enter into another conversation—a conversation that power-as-enforcement may not want to have." (Ricardo Dominguez in *Hyperallergic*, 2012)

In which poetry becomes the dissolver, destabilizing the line between "legality" or "illegality."

*

Text of bliss ... to bring to a crisis [their] relation with language.

*

"To put it simply, a poem means one thing and says another."
(Michael Riffaterre, *Semiotics of Poetry*, 1)

*

Mantras, those chanted enchantments, originated in Vedic poetry. The Japanese word for mantra, 真言 (shingon), means "true word."

In addition to magic, one purpose of a 魔ntra is to create internal changes, rather than outward. This can be accomplished by calling upon an external power, or by the calming, focusing action of repetition.

*

Gate gate para gate para sam gate bodhi svaha
Gone, gone to the other shore, liberated, hail!

*

Plants used for limpias, spiritual cleansings: Santa Maria, pirul, poleo, shuyu rosas de cerro, laurel grande, romero, ruda, wandug, marco cali, cholo valiente, ...

*

For now, I want the book to be a crisis:

"If my freedom were not in the book, where would it be?
If my book were not my freedom, what would it be?
Truth cannot but be violent. There is no peaceable truth. [...]
The violence of the book is turned against the book: battle without mercy."
(Edmond Jabès, *The Book of Margins*, 5)

A crisis of bliss—I will write my way from here to there, or not.

WORKING WITH POWER WORDS

This is an exercise that introduces the practice of building and infusing energy into language through repetition (ritual) and intention (personal power). Here, we'll play with identifying and building relationship with words or phrases of power.

★ Begin by setting aside at least twenty minutes for this experiment. Find a space where you can have privacy and not have to worry about making too much noise. This is a good one to do at your altar!

★ Once you're in your comfortable space, make a list of ten words that feel potent or powerful to you. These can be qualities you'd like to experience, your favorite colors, trees, or animals, the name of a place you feel connected to, a favorite crystal or rock—anything you feel drawn to. Or you can use words from the list below.

★ Choose one word from the list, set a timer for one minute, and repeat that word for the full minute. Say it aloud at different volumes: try both whispering the word and shouting it or saying it in increasing or decreasing volumes. Say it while sitting, standing, or lying down. Say it rapidly and say it slowly.

★ Notice how it feels to say this word in these different ways. Is there something you notice in your body? A temperature change—does it feel warm or cool? Other sensations?

★ Notice if there are images that arise—these can be smells, visual images, memories, tastes, etc.

★ Once the full minute is up, take three minutes to free-write about your experience repeating that word.

★ Choose another word and repeat the process of saying it, noticing sensations, and free-writing. If a word starts to feel overwhelming or uncomfortable in a way you don't like (meaning in a way your intuition or body does not feel any curiosity about or desire to encounter), simply stop, take a few clearing breaths, and choose a word that brings more calm to your system.

★ After you have repeated this with two to three words, take five to ten minutes to write or start a poem using the words you have chosen.

Word list

ocean	ease	sugar	flicker	panther
power	cedar	whisk	stalk	blossom
snake	flame	earth	purpose	peace
dahlia	eagle	night	teddy bear	roots
justice	grace	worm	soften	turn

Articulating the Undercurrent

DOMINIQUE MATTI

i.

call it our wildness then / we are lost from the field /
of flowers, we become / a field of flowers
—LUCILLE CLIFTON, "ROOTS"

The summer I refined my ability to speak with the spirits of ancestors, flowers, and trees, death was on the tongue and the nontongue of everything talking. The city was all smoke and teargas and sickness, and the fatalities were climbing and climbing still. I did not know what to do but to cultivate life and tend to my beloved dead and dying. I offered drops of my blood to the soil freely so that it would not take it of its own accord. I watered the seeds I'd sown in four half rows and sang to them to curry favor. I planted only those that I knew my ancestors had known, and I introduced myself to the sprouts as kin. I was the great-granddaughter of the friend of their great grand-spirit, and so the spirits in my garden afforded me a sense of familiarity. Its blooms grew chatty. They opened themselves up to me and they fed my hunger for their secrets. I was humble and voracious in the quiet of their noise, an eager and devoted student.

Animals began to regard me as if I was no longer an intruder on the land, but someone who belonged where I was. This was a foreign sensation. Squirrels were still in my presence. Butterflies rode my shoulder. Spiders met my gaze with their many-eyed glances. I was welcomed, for we shared a common calling (to be what we are), and we shared our common friends, and our enemies. The ancestral spirits rooting for my survival had so persistently loved them too. And the systems seeking to destroy me were coming for us both. In my garden's microcosm, small but vast, I had conjured up a sense of the inextricable nature of us all. We were in the universal overlap, and we shared our medicine there. Like how my great-grandmother's nature spared the spiders in her home, and their webs packed the wounds of her children.

I had researched extensively what mythmakers, herbalists, scientists, and mystics said that my plants could do, but once we had forged a bond I became increasingly fixed on hearing it from them directly. I devoted myself to a practice of creating flower essences—a spiritual medicine-making ritual by which one forges a relationship with the spirit of a flower, makes an offering, and asks the flower to share an offering of its own. One must wait, listen, notice, feel, intuit, and discern what that offering might be. The offering is transmitted by placing the flower in or above a clear bowl of water, where it imprints its energetic signature. This signature is its medicine, its medicine is its nature, and the water is a conduit or vessel for it. When the water is bottled, preserved, and taken as a remedy, one is essentially allowing the flower to bring its signature forth through them. It gifts the willing participant a portion of its nature by facilitating their recognition of where in their own spirit that nature has always been possible.

Poetry, for me, is an essence-making process. The words serve as the clear bowl of water, a conduit for communication between the mouthless subterranean in me and that which has been buried, unarticulated, in you. Poems are not the words themselves but what the words transmit. Not the thunderclap, but how our bodies respond to the boom. How the storm utilizes the thunderclap to enter us. Poetry is not the scientific report purporting how aromatic plants impact the vagus nerve, but the slow exhaling shoulder-drop after a deep huff of Lavender. A full body amen. A ritual of replication and noticing. A willingness to witness and be borne witness to. A sacred exchange. Poetry is an instrument I use to deconstruct the thin borders between myself and all that is. A portal to the overlapping center of the divine Venn diagram of creation. The use of language to speak not mouth to mind, but spirit to spirit.

At my mom's house a few years ago, in stacks of old gel pen–riddled composition books and wide-lined beginner notepad pages, I found the earliest evidence of both my propensity for poetry and my propensity for attuning to the underground. On one page, which dates me at age six, I wrote in the rudimentary scrawl of someone just learning to hold a pencil: *I am a girl who can see thi[n]gs that are not ther[e]*. And on countless others, I etched out my first simple poems. The concurrent manifestation of these gifts rendered them inextricable from one another, facilitated the potentiality of each other. They asserted themselves in me as a necessity to translate what was not readily apparent to those I encountered. In one hand, I held the capacity to hear the language of the undercurrent, and with the other hand, I was afforded the capacity to speak it myself. I learned that it was possible to *feel* what one could not otherwise know. And that I could transmit feeling where rational explanation failed, by using poetry like a lyre—plucking invisible energetic strings. I discovered that where no one would cry for me, my poetry could conjure easy tears. And when my spirit could not represent itself in mundane gesture, it could rise up and shout in verse. I fell fast in love with symbol and rhythm and pattern and repetition and the way they speak to the body and spirit beyond an ordinary tongue. Still, it took two more decades for me to become consciously aware of the two-headed nature of these practices. It took attempts to communicate with that which was not human.

I first began speaking deliberately to natural and ancestral spirits because I wanted to share what I could not otherwise share and know what I could not otherwise know. I doubted the viability of entrusting the magnitude of my internal experience and unrelenting curiosity to the limited scope that my species and mortality confined me to. I presumed that spirits could afford me access to what was too large or too small for my embodied eye. All around me I could sense an environment populated by infinite latent witnesses and onlookers, and I desired to be in conversation with them. So I set about becoming fluid in their language, assisted by the ways in which energy transmission had become second nature through writing.

The Doctrine of Signatures is an ancient cross-cultural theory that says, in short, that every plant possesses visible clues that allude to its particular healing (or harming) qualities. In romantic terms it's the notion that every sentient thing is venturing to convey what it carries inside it, if only for the sake of being holistically recognized. Those without the luxury (or menace) of words *wear* their poetry, dress in intricate arrangements of symbols meant to help us to know what they otherwise couldn't express. Like how the coiling tendrils of the Passionflower vine hint at its propensity for easing spiraling thoughts. And there's the translucent moon-white pallor of Ghost Pipe, whose bloom lifts its face to the sun, refuses it, and lowers its gaze back to the dirt. Its physical expression serves as an elaborate nature-writ metaphor for how its spirit might help us to process our sunken grief, our deep-down dead, all that the light does not touch in us.

ii.

that leaf / pick up / the sharp / green stem /
try to feel me feel you
—LUCILLE CLIFTON, "OUT OF BODY"

After a year or so of studying plant medicine with the Doctrine of Signatures, what began as simple observation and ritual practice of noticing (What color is this plant? What shape? How do I feel when I am with it? Where does it grow? What does it favor?), rapidly evolved into more direct forms of communication. And in retrospect it feels in exact right accordance that this was facilitated by my pen. It happened in August of 2020, that summer of endings and openings. I was in an herbalism course where we were encouraged to sit with the plants we were working with and discern what we could about them with our own intuitive devices. We had been given journals to take notes, and I was lying on the ground with a brown paper bag of Peppermint when I felt the strong urge to write. I put my first mind behind me and transcribed what came as it came. It was this:

> Once upon a time there was a girl. And the girl was her grandmother
> and her grandmother and her grandmother was the girl. I am not the
> only one. When she wept she cried other women's tears. Breathed
> everybody's breath. Ancestral streams and breezes. Dreams of her body
> were in other women's visions. Bleeding blood of other women's blood.
> Expand. Open up to it. Welcoming. Holding. It is possible. You are.
> Believe in it. What do you do with your believing? I can only say what
> I know. When you move you move me. Teach. Learn. Awake. Alive.
> In unison. At once. Forever. Expand. Beyond it. Inside it. Of it. Are it.
> Open. Welcoming. Holding. In mint I smell a river. Cool water. Deep.
> Where do you go when it carries you?

I did and did not write these words. My personal revisions of it were rejected by something else acting through me. The words were offered up to me by the mint and I gave them to the mint in return. The poem was established in convergence. It was a middle of the Venn diagram poem, a poem at the crossroads of our being. This cowriting, like my earliest experiences with verse, cracked open my sense of possibility for what it meant to be in relationship with the world around me. I wondered, what else might speak to me this way? Or listen?

iii.

> *It is the life thing in us /*
> *that will not let us die. / even in death's hand*
> —LUCILLE CLIFTON, "ROOTS"

One month later, in September, I was grooming my garden plot when I noticed Datura inoxia breaking form from my curated rows. It had reached across the dusty aisle and put its mouth to Rabbit Tobacco's ear. Datura (colloquially known as Angel's Trumpet) is lethally poisonous, but its essence is known for helping the dying to honor what is coming.

And Rabbit Tobacco, a Down South medicine, is known for its ability to aid in communication with the dead. Basking in my newfound capacity to discern between my own internal narrative and the other-voice poetry of the plants, I asked them for permission to eavesdrop on their conversation. I was permitted, contingent on my understanding that I was not a part of it. So I sat, and waited, and noticed, and felt, and listened.

They spoke with immense levity to one another about death, about how little we (humans) know of it, how what we have seen is a sliver of what it is. How our fear of the small bit we are aware of restricts our movements to the extent that we squander the glory of life itself. How death and life continue each other, how both are and neither is the sinister underbelly of the other and how both are and neither is the beaming upside. They identified themselves as stewards of the gateway. And it was all very casual and bright between them. But I was gripped by a penetrative panic and paranoia. I blurted an inquiry into why they were talking about this with *me* as audience—were they trying to pre-console me for my own death? As quick as I'd uttered it, they shot right back: *Not every encounter is about what we are seeking to do for you—sometimes it's what your presence can do for us.*

And yet, by the middle of the next month, I began to contend with what felt like an excruciating marathon of the deaths of people I knew. In October I was rattled by the death of a young community member. In November, I lost my Pop Pop, and the morning after his funeral came the news that my beloved cousin had passed. The next month I lost an old friend. The next month I lost another. I felt brutalized by loss and forsaken by the spirits who I felt should have helped me to stop it all somehow, to beat back death itself. I became afraid to check my Facebook for fear of being notified of another.

Death felt so frequent and prevalent that I began to interpret the Death card presenting itself routinely in my tarot spreads as quite literally indicative of more death. I felt startled into the awareness of death's ever-present intimacy with life, and I did not know where to seek shelter. In tandem with the persistent hum of all that fear, grief was threatening to submerge me. I was urgently required by my life, and so I did my best to bury the grief instead. But where the grief grew roots underground, anger shot up like crimson flowers. By the dictate of the Doctrine of Signatures, red suggests a remedy for something bleeding.

iv.

I am saying / I am trying to say /
from my mouth / but oh baby / there is no mouth
—LUCILLE CLIFTON, "OUT OF BODY"

I wanted it witnessed. But what words, in ordinary conversation, could be utilized to capture the immensity? Which would do? Longing, despairing, hoping, missing, doubting, waiting, holding, aching, bargaining, regretting, worrying, pleading, wanting and wanting and wanting and wishing I could but I can't? None sufficed. Not even grieving. And so I rode routine laps on my bike through the cemetery, with volumes of poetry in my backpack, which I'd rely on for weeping beneath a towering pine. I cleaved to the magic of poetry, which was my prayer and my prayer answered, and my dead conspired with nature to make poetry for me too.

They sent symbols to me in waking life, allusions expressed in synchronicity—my brother, aunt, and I all sharing evidence on the same day of ladybugs insisting upon us. And the memory risen up of my child shouting my attention over to the ladybug perched in the center of the door to my Pop Pop's house on the night of the day we said good-bye. Visitations in dreams, that ethereal poetry of the unconscious, consoled me. In one, my cousin sat next to me at his own funeral, with a drink in hand, and asked me if I wanted one too. He invited me to a room adjacent to the rows of somber pews where we could watch sports together if we wanted. Another time, the obscure song I wrote down while listening to a rerun of my dead friend's radio show (just to hear her voice) appeared in the episode of a TV show I put on later that night. I did not bother to analyze what any of it meant because I felt the message it had infused into my spirit—that I was not alone. As with a flower essence. As with a poem. As with language before language, the old ways of speaking. A bit of the nature of everything collaborating to hold that within me which was otherwise invisible, unknown, unsupported.

Eventually, I began employing the same tactics taught to me by the mint. I'd sit at my ancestor altar, light a candle, longing just to talk, and ask my dead to write with me. While they often spoke in the distorted format of a disjointed monologue, a loved one once directly chose poetry. Feeling desperate to understand where he was, how he was, I asked him to tell me with my pen, and he offered me this:

> I am not who I used to be. I used to be someone you might recognize, and now I hardly recognize myself. I am in the dark. The dark is not in me. There's a difference. You'll understand in your own time but that time is not for some time. I came to tell you that yes I love you and yes I am not forgotten or forgetting you, but maybe a poem is a better idea.

> The grass whispers over the meadow
> and the fox is waiting
> and the birds chirp on
> and the sun still shines and so on

> I can't talk about beauty when I know what happens to us all.
> even if it had its beauty too.
> even if in the dark there is a light.
> like all the poets say.
> even if I am the light.
> though I do not emanate.
> even if we are all unprotected.
> even if I miss some body.
> without my own
> being. / being
> is not easy.
> I respect that.

Dom, I am with you when you can't feel anything but your own anger. I am with you when your eyes well up with tears. you don't have to feel my hand to touch my hand, for my hand to touch you. you don't have to have a great shining moment. spirit is all subtlety. the loud moments are the life in you. let it all be. there's no other way. thank you. I love you. goodnight.

V.

And what shall we do, we who did not die?
—JUNE JORDAN, "SOME OF US DID NOT DIE"

In the months since the summer that all the plants in my garden, and the trees in the woods, and the poetry in my volumes, and the owls in my dreams delivered sermon after sermon on death and the afterlife to the pit of my spirit—I have largely regarded it all as an equipping for the following season of losing and then finding again. And maybe so, in some ways, it was a conspiracy of care, but what care was my portion to send back out into the overlap? What good word was I meant to spread?

I have wondered and wondered to myself about the quick admonition of the Datura flower. What can I provide for those who so many have not yet learned to hear? How can I make an offering of my presence in underground conversations? What is my service as one who stewards the messages of the dead, of the human and more-than-human undercurrent? As one who deals in the transmission of medicine from the root to the root? As a gardener? As a poet?

I once read that at the core of much trauma is a sense of having been skipped over, bypassed, denied a customary regard for one's being. That's a poem my spirit knows by heart. Still, it stands to reason that at the core of much healing is a sense of noticing and being noticed by eyes that look favorably upon you. Eyes that see you as a precious and integral part of something that they too are a part of. A gaze that affirms that you are seen, you are known, you are held, you belong, you are not alone here. And there are living and dead and seashell and Mugwort and river and rain and starling and jupiter and moon and Sycamore and ancestor and a legion of familiar stranger conjurer poets who are willing to serve as a community of loving witnesses. They are our cowriters of what has come before, what is yet to come, and the unseen already here—or in the words of my six-year-old self: what is "not there."

Awakening of Stones: Results

LISBETH WHITE

at mile 2,219
the Southwest desert is stretching
long & ashy-brown as my thigh

from this distance
the ocean 452 miles away
from this dust floor
the ocean 166 million years gone
still salting the back of my throat

the way west
is a ceremony of names

    morbid one may think
    or naive

on her grave i murmured Great-Grandma Marie
a secret up from the Florida coast
in Mobile there is Cudjo Lewis
Oluale, Oluale, i whisper

through Arkansas through Oklahoma
words and people in the grasses
wafting waist high in litany:
Quapaw, Tonkawa, Yscani

soon i will say Bears Ears
soon i will say yellow-faced bee
soon i will say Monotropa uniflora

the ghost plant

whose medicine puts us
beside our pain
that we may utter
a name for its shape & call it
something other
than ourselves

these are pathways
one must be laid bare upon
one must be flayed open
to hear

i scrabble up granite Crestone
to listen in clear air
burst the plump promise
in my fingertips
& call the blood
sweetness

but it must be known—
i am no woman of nostalgia

never was i speaking the dead
but naming those who lived

why bother calling memory
what is altogether
sovereign from the mind
& comes winging out
from the ribs
like a swift

what leaves must be sung to
as it goes

we must let unfurl
the root of our bodies
span down   across   up

the crossroads as they say

& feel the ground
beneath

INVOKING RADICAL IMAGINATION

Enchantment: The Liberatory Gift of Wonder

LISBETH WHITE

Enchantment

noun

1. *A feeling of great pleasure; delight*
2. *The state of being under a spell; magic*

I have been writing poems about owls. A lot of poems about owls. Almost a poem a day about owls. Many are very short—a haiku or simple sentence. Most often, lately, they are transcriptions (or perhaps more accurately, a translation) of their sounds. There are two who dwell in the same woods in which I dwell, and I often hear their conversation.

Who-who-whoooo-ooooo. Or *Broo-brooooroo, broooroooroo.*

I cannot resist calling my partner from the other room to press our ears against the screen door when I hear the faintest hoot. My friends and family members are beginning to joke about the obsessiveness of my "owl report," which consists of the time of the last hooting, how often they may have spoken in one night cycle, or a particularly unique utterance.

One evening, there was a sound like a burbling, angry brook that bubbled out from the trees. A sound I had never before contemplated as an animal sound, yet there it was erupting from a feathered body onto the air, my ears eager to catch it.

There is a kind of rhetoric toward obsession in the study of poetry. It appears often and again in poetry workshops and classes, chapbook coaching, and manuscript critiques. I've witnessed throughout poetry academia an invitation into, and certain pride taken in, ownership of obsession (obsession, in this case, referencing the domination of one's thoughts or feelings by a persistent idea, image, desire, etc.). There's an encouragement to dive headlong into the topics one ruminates on, churns, and repeats. There's an encouragement to lean in to what preoccupies, to perceive all the angles with every sense available, to let the repetition of what is perceived become its own form and function. In this way, the repetition finds pockets of rhythm, overlaps and gaps, and becomes an incantation of sorts. The so-called obsession eventually becomes a ritual recitation, in the form of a single poem or collection.

I have always been down for this rhetoric, being of a temperament and astrological sign that appreciates a good emotional dive. So when I entered into the world of poetry writing, I reveled in the invitation and permission to be *obsessed*. I wrote into every subtlety and nuance I perceived about a particular moment or theme. I wrote long and short, experimented with formalism and free verse, with rhythm and sound. I was writing about very personal traumatic experiences at the time, and allowing myself to consider these experiences worthy of such attention was the beginning of a healing. To engage in a practice of deep attention felt like a new liberation of sorts.

It also felt profoundly familiar, bone-level familiar, anciently familiar.

When I was a child, I could gaze out my bedroom window for hours. There were four trees outside, one evergreen near the front corner of the house and three young maples on the side. The twist and turn of maple leaves in the breeze, the wolf-shaped shadow on the sidewalk made by the stiff branches of evergreen in early afternoon—this attention to detail earned me a reputation for being at once compulsive and spacey, singularly distracted. Yet, when I began to study poetry again, and when I began to practice ritual work in earnest, it was this very attention to detail that enhanced both practices.

As a child given to dreamlike states, my perception of the natural world was sensory and expansive. My relationship to it felt, and still feels, as tangible and alive as any relationship I have with human beings. I am not alone in this—many of us pursued this study of connection as we entered life. It is actually a very common inclination to engage with the subtle energies of the world. We tend to receive most permission to engage this sense of wonder and enchantment as children, through play and the creative freedom of imagination. Even fettered within various expressions of repression (poverty, war, the ensuing traumas), there are often occasions of wonderment, moments when the imaginal breaks us into a painful and sacred longing toward what might be possible beyond the horror we are experiencing.

We begin here, and if we are taught that it is acceptable to continue to pay attention, we may hone this skill of open-eyed awareness into an adeptness and faculty for engaging with these subtle energies of the world, for relating and conversing, for channeling them into magic and healing. Some of us carry this talent from birth forward, having been supported in the ritual and ceremonial life that allows the energies of the natural world to converse freely with us. Some of us, like myself, felt it in our bodies as children, matriculated through a human- and commerce-centered "growing up," and needed to recover the knowledge again later in life, as we began to reclaim our original wholeness.

In the study of poetics, this sort of presenced attention might be called obsession. In magic, it is called enchantment.

And what a wondrous word. *Enchantment.* Even the simple act of typing it conjures images of twilight spellcasting and sirens swaying travelers off their intended course. It evokes adventure, the titillating drive of desire, and the creation of a new something material, tangible, lived. (Does this also sound like poem-making?) It evokes the processes and rules of alchemy, that seemingly magical process of transmutation, of turning a base metal, or experience, into gold.

While a primary understanding of alchemy orients in the physical realm (the chemistry of transforming one material object such as lead into another one like gold), like all magical practices the study of alchemy begins as an internal one. Inner alchemy holds the intention of transforming consciousness for the purpose of personal and collective evolution. All successful alchemy requires three elements: (1) a substance to be transformed; (2) a container to hold the alchemical reaction; and (3) energy. In the case of inner alchemies, the container to hold the transformation is awareness itself. Our attention, and how it is held, creates the very container for change.

This is why there is such power in following our creative obsessions, those relentless curiosities. Our awareness—our focus, our attention—becomes the vessel in which the possibility of a new knowingness can arise. As in ritual work, with poetry we begin with the tools at hand. The obsession or idea of what we want to write is the initial substance to be transformed. Our attention to it is the container creating the space for transformation. The energy brought in to spark the change, which in turn develops and informs the nature of the change itself … well, that all depends on the quality of our attention.

Not all attention is love and there is great danger for harm in conflating the two. Writing through personal and collective trauma, even in my work as a healer, I am constantly learning this. There are many ways even our genuine curiosity can lean toward appropriation if we enter an experience with the desire to alter, fix, predict, or interpret, rather than witness and accompany. These qualities of attention express through our exchanges in the realm of subtle energy. The how and why of our approach to an experience become apparent in the outcome.

When I began these owl poems, I admit I succumbed to the unexacting charm of pastoral poetry. Pastoral poems, that large umbrella term the poetic academy offers as the primary example of nature poetry, feature an idealized and romanticized vision of connection to the natural world. This phenomena of romanticization is indicative of the underlying ease of objectification that permeates our cultural awareness. It required little of my true attention to wander a landscape of preconceived notions about owls and what it was they were doing in those woods. I could hear their calling and suppose nearly anything. I could project what I wished was true about what I was witnessing—say, for instance, that they were looking for each other after a long day of separate nesting, rather than shouting out the coordinates of hiding mice. While the former makes for a lovely poem, it also collapses and flattens the vessel for meaning into an autocratic one.

Whether I am conscious of it all the time or not, the same happens as I prepare a spellwork or I write about the life and world in which I am living. An overbearing or already-knowing quality of attention doesn't lead to a truly innovative transformation, but rather a nearby and comfortable shift in circumstance. This may result in a poem that is seductive and perhaps a spell too. But will we have been truly moved?

One of my poet-comrades shared emphatically that he didn't want to read a poem about a tree unless the poet sat with that tree long enough to be changed by it.

"Did you let that tree make you into something different? No? Then don't waste my time."

I laughed at his stark delivery but felt a tugging memory of those trees outside my childhood window. What it felt like to see them with such curiosity and awe. How my own body would calm or excite with a shift in the light. How I never knew what I would perceive until I sat in the still center of myself and opened my senses completely. Only then might I see something of the trees.

One of the first entries into the practice of magic is the relearning of enchantment. But why be enchanted? Why lend oneself to a way of being that insinuates surrender, or being caught up beyond your control?

In many versions of the Tarot, the card that opens the deck, and thus the spiritual journey of transformation, is The Fool. The Fool is often portrayed with childlike innocence, so captivated by something in their surroundings they may walk right off a cliff. Yet it is this very quality of enchanted attention that moves The Fool toward the cliff, the edge of what is known, into a new beyond. The Fool is also sometimes referred to as the Universe's favorite child. The Powers Unseen delight in the delight of The Fool, and so all tools required for the journey through transformation are gifted with generosity and grace.

This is not a way of being that caste and capitalist cultures tolerate, relying instead on domination, prescription, and exploitation to achieve one's desires. Systems of oppression operate most functionally in what witch and writer Lisa Fazio coins "Predictability Supremacy." Predictability Supremacy can be conceived as the tight space of a closed system, rigid and patterned ways of thinking, feeling, and expressing, in which any perceived deviance is severely punished. For me, this is exactly the motivation I need to allow myself to come again into an attentiveness that is earnest and generous. My enchantment—my re-enchantment—with the world as a whole becomes my very resistance against isolation, exploitation, and alienation.

True transformation, true power, does not exist in a vacuum, but in a space with many other energies, many other beings, many other knowings. Or else there is no material, physical or psychic, to transform. There *is* wonderment in enchantment. It belies innocence, by which I mean both vulnerability and a willingness toward that vulnerability. It softens the rigid edges of thinking to make room for play and the seepage of surprise. The relearning of enchantment activates expansion as we must stretch the container of our perception beyond what is physically and materially known. We must be open to awe.

This is how we enter the transformative arts.

If poetic obsession is held as a practice of enchantment, there is spellwork that arises. While enchanted, the poem becomes a vessel, energy summoned and held in the container of line. If the work of healing is held with a practice of enchantment, there is a potential for recovery of loss, whether that loss is of power, connection to the soul, or a type of innocence. While enchanted, when I write about even the most tender suffering and ache of the world, the writing itself becomes an application of love in the form of deep attention and care that touches the page. If the work of social and spiritual justice is held with a practice of enchantment, there opens a portal for all ways of beingness and knowingness to be present, to engage, and to be witnessed. While enchanted, even the slow alchemy of revolution might be graced with something that could resemble play, and feel even a bit like delight.

Sometimes the owl poems become long nocturnes. This happens when I hear the owls calling to each other at times of dimming and dawning, at dusk and in the earliest morning light. The sounds at these times have a hollow throated-ness, a roundness like a vessel, as if the calls are curving a space in the air.

These are the times of day when it becomes most apparent our world is turning, that light and dark come and go with a rhythm we are embedded in, encoded with. These are the times I find myself alternatively in easeful appreciation of being present to witness the transition— the sighing sunset, the beckoning sunrise—and discomfited by the shift urging me along to a new state of being. It is time to prepare a way for being in the night. Or, it is time to prepare a way for entering the new day.

These are the times when the owls send out their voices and I stretch my listening for them. The call-and-response of their soundings begin to overlap, creating a rhythm without break. One long, pulsing incantation through the shifting of the light. I stretch, I extend, I become expanded to hear them. I open my hearing to allow as much of the sound as possible. I hold it with wonder, and wait.

WRITING EXERCISE FOR REENCHANTMENT

* Set aside about twenty-five minutes dedicated to this practice.

* Gather your writing paraphernalia and sit in a place where you are either outside or near a window.

* For the first three minutes, gaze out at your surroundings. Don't try to take particular notice of any one thing, just let your senses and attention wander. Spend a moment imagining each sense you have access to as gently stretching or extending to receive the subtle nuances of what is around you. What is present as sound, taste, touch, smell, sight? If you begin to feel overwhelmed or flooded in any way, place a hand on your chest and bring your breath back into your body until you feel grounded again.

* Take one minute to write down any two or three phrases or words that come to you.

* For the next three minutes, see where your attention is drawn and allow it to linger there. Again, engage as much of your senses as feels comfortable, and imagine them as a gentle light hovering just near where your attention is drawn. Try not to zero in. Rather, hold this focus as open as possible, almost like a wide-angle lens.

* Take the next full minute to again write two or three phrases or words that come to you.

* For the next three minutes, close your eyes or hold a soft gaze and summon a memory of tenderness and wonder. It may be a memory of a beloved childhood pet, a new experience with a trusted loved one, or simply a warm, soft feeling of expansion in the chest. Connect to this sense in whatever way works best for you.

★ Take the next full minute to write the two or three phrases or words that arise.

★ For the next three minutes, gaze once again at your surroundings while allowing this sense of wonder to remain present. If you need to take a moment to reengage this feeling, go ahead and return to the sense-memory for a few moments before taking in the scene currently around you again.

★ Use the remainder of the time to write whatever you wish about your experience, or to shape a poem.

★ Close this practice by thanking all the elements of place and beings that were present to your noticing.

Poetry as Prayer

HYEJUNG KOOK

Listen. What do you hear in your stillness? In a moment of deep feeling, what have you heard from your innermost self? Who did you turn to?

Who, if I cried out, would hear me among the angels'
hierarchies? and even if one of them pressed me
suddenly against his heart: I would be consumed
in that overwhelming existence. For beauty is nothing
but the beginning of terror, which we still are just able to endure,
and we are so awed because it serenely disdains
to annihilate us. Every angel is terrifying.
And so I hold myself back and swallow the call-note
of my dark sobbing. Ah, whom can we ever turn to
in our need?[1]

Poetry, like prayer, comes out of urgency and necessity and at times des-peration. Both involve a calling out from the heart, addressed to an Other with the hope of being heard. In Christianity, the invocation in prayer is usually directed toward God, angels, or saints, asking for assistance. Here, Rilke does not actually call upon the divine; he poses the invocation as a hypothetical, partly from an uncertainty of being heard, and partly from the terror of an angel who "serenely disdains to annihilate us." And yet while he declares "I hold myself back and swallow the call-note of my

---

[1] From "The First Elegy" by Rainer Maria Rilke, translated by Stephen Mitchell, *Duino Elegies and the Sonnets to Orpheus* (New York: Vintage, 2009)

dark sobbing," he persists in calling out, not to an angel but to the reader, to himself, committing his words to paper. His prayer is the poem.

I grew up without prayer as part of my daily life, but there was poetry, which I always loved and memorized for school and pleasure. After immigrating to the United States, I didn't go to church, but I did have godparents and attended Catholic preschool, which must be where I memorized my first poem, the bedtime prayer "Now I lay me down to sleep / I pray the Lord my soul will keep / And if I die before I wake / I pray the Lord my soul will take." Here is an echo of the terror that Rilke speaks of in his poem, the possibility of annihilation, which I sensed but mostly dismissed until my maternal grandfather passed away. He was a living treasure of Seoul, a master craftsman of Korean traditional furniture, particularly 나전 질기 (najeon jilgi), mother-of-pearl inlay work. I grew up with his furniture, and we went back to visit every few years. He was the model of what an artist was as well as beloved family, but because of my limited Korean, I'd never had a real conversation with him, and now it was too late.

When he died, I was nineteen, a sophomore at Harvard studying English and American literature. The only tangible thing of his I had was a jewelry box, too precious to keep in my college dorm. I had writing aspirations but had been twice rejected from poetry workshops, and the ability to write creatively disappeared in the face of my first true loss. I felt ghostly, haunting the dark subterranean levels of Widener and Pusey libraries, turning on the lights to look through the stacks, searching for something, words that might ground me when my own were gone. And in my wandering, I came across Felix Grendon's edition of Anglo-Saxon charms. Here was language of origin, one of the wellsprings of modern English, vaguely familiar but mostly bewildering. Here was poetry that was magical, charged with the intention to heal, and in my grief, it resonated deeply.

While I didn't engage in rhetorical analysis of the charms at the time, I could still sense the structuredness of the metrical charms, so opposed to the incoherence of my feelings. The foreignness of Anglo-Saxon was an intellectual puzzle that also helped distract and occupy me. Twelve metrical charms have survived, among them the "Nine Herbs Charm." A spell against poison, the poem begins with an invocation of each herb that is both ritualized and intimate. Like prayer, the poem calls upon external powers for assistance, and I sensed then and now a yearning to bridge distance, between the self and the called-upon power as well as between the hurt and healed state, built into the structure of the charm. For example, waybread (plantain) is invoked this way:

7 Ond þū, Wegbrāde,   wyrta mōdor,
8 ēastan openo,   innan mihtigu;
9 ofer ðē cræto curran,   ofer ðē cwēne reodan,
10 ofer ðē brȳde brvo   dedon, ofer ðē fearras fnærdon.
11 Eallum þū þon wiðstōnde   and wiðstunedest;
12 swā ðū wiðstonde   āttre and onflyge
13 and þæm lāðan   þe geond lond fereð.

And, you, waybread,   mother of herbs,
open to the east,   mighty within;
over you carts rolled,   over you women rode
over you brides cried out,   over you bulls snorted.
All you then withstood,   and were crushed;
So you withstand   poison and contagion
and the loathsome one   who through the land fares.

Waybread is addressed informally in second person with "þu" ("thou"), followed by the epithet "mother of herbs" and brief descriptive phrases. This pattern follows for all nine herbs. "Thou" sounds formal to our ears, but the term was originally intimate, reserved for family and friends. Anglo-Saxon prosody is characterized by caesura and alliteration (which included vowel sounds and so absorbs modern-day assonance), a state of physical division and aural similarity. The alliterative sound falls on an accented syllable and also needs to bridge the caesura of the line. Sound literally spans the caesura, a sort of sonic stitching of the break. The syntax of the poem also works with and in contrast to the two parts created by the caesura. We have parallel structure and the repetition of "over" in lines 9 and 10, but we also have the appearance of triples providing counterpoint—"wiðstandan" in different conjugations, the triple threat of poison and contagion and "the loathsome one."

After all nine herbs are invoked, the poem declares their power over nine poisons and nine contagions and nine who fled glory, a reiteration and expansion of the power mentioned in lines 12 and 13. The repeated appearance of threes and nines, a tripled triple, clearly connects to the sense of three as sacred and powerful, which occurs across cultures. The poem doesn't simply describe a situation but like prayer, uses invocation, sound, and repetition in order to bring focus to something the petitioner hopes to influence with more-than-human intercession. Anglo-Saxon charms are poems with a magical, or in other words, practical application of language, to address a situation that needs attending.

Yet poetry that doesn't clearly invoke a god or saint or nonhuman power can still work in a prayer-like mode, calling us readers to attention and also charging language with powerful intention. An example of such a poem is Lucille Clifton's "blessing the boats" in which she uses address and repetition of sound and image to imbue her blessing with potency.[2] The poem comprises four statements that begin with "may," opening with the following phrase.

may the tide
that is entering even now
the lip of our understanding

We begin in a space of nature with the tide, but then "the lip of our understanding" shifts us into a metaphorical space that is simultaneously embodied. The address of the poem is ostensibly to the boats, but the first pronoun she uses is "our," which intimates "you and I," and I feel the address encompasses both the boat and the reader. With the lines "certain that it will / love your back   may you," I feel even more that the boat is also the reader, and Clifton is calling a blessing upon us all.

The repetitions continue to occur with more frequency in the closing four and a half lines of the poem with "you … your … you," and "water" repeated across a line break. Sharper enjambments and decreased time between each "may" also create an increasing sense of urgency. The poem then closes with the briefest "may" statement.

may you in your innocence
sail through this to that

The indeterminacy of "this to that" allows all of us to be part of the blessing, to be offered the assurance that we can make it through whatever it is that we are struggling to make it through. And the sonic qualities of that deceptively simple last line—monosyllabic, trochaic, the repetition of "th"—increases the quality of power and certainty. The poem is in the subjunctive mood, in a space of wishing just as prayer is, and yet with each "may"

---

[2] To read the full poem, see www.poetryfoundation.org/poems/58816/blessing-the -boats.

statement arriving more quickly, with gentle assuredness, Clifton somehow goes beyond mere wishfulness and toward bringing her blessing into reality by the power of her utterance. The experience of reading her poem gives me fortitude, and so, the piece feels like prayer and prayer fulfilled.

So far I have been looking at the intersection of poetry and prayer mainly by way of formal understanding, examining texts in English and looking for patterns and principles. Both use address, invocation, naming, and repetitions of sound and word, weaving a sonic spell with the intention of bringing something into reality. The formulaic aspect of prayer that relies on forms passed down through generations, where there are specific words and procedures with how we offer up our appeals, has its own heft. Looking at a text carried forward for years, even millennia, knowing it has been pored over by others and then to pore over it myself, adds weight as I see how it is made and then apply those ways of making to my own writing. If this is how an Anglo-Saxon charm worked, then I can make a poem-prayer-spell the "correct" way. Part of the power of prayer comes from repetition through time, where repetition itself grants faith and force, knowing we are part of lineage to some ancient origin as a source of strength.

But a reliance on forms and formulas alone only goes so far. When we are in extremity, when we are calling out in desperation, there is a place where the only thing that will work is to make anew, where no old form has the answer. All words seem to fail, but silence would swallow us whole. When my grandfather passed, retreating into Anglo-Saxon charms was only a temporary escape and reprieve. Eventually, I had to step forward into darkness, hands outstretched, into the not-knowing—the only way to emerge was to go through.

Listen: I need to begin again. I need to go to my own origin and lineages, the places I falter and feel uncertain. Can you hear it? 내 마음의 소리, the sound of my heart, beating faster and faster.

My first language was Korean. I was born in Korea and came to the States when I was eleven months old. I lost my fluency when I started kindergarten, but I still remember my parents telling me stories and singing children's songs in Korean. The first prayers I heard, though I can't remember them, were Buddhist, living in my maternal grandfather's house when I was a baby. In 1988, when we visited for the first time since leaving, my sister and I slept in my grandparents' room, and every morning I would wake and then fall back asleep listening to my grandmother chanting a Buddhist text. I couldn't understand most of the words, so her prayer was mainly sound and feeling, like music, and her voice rising and falling would carry me back to sleep. I am reminded that a lullaby is a kind of prayer-spell, our caretakers fervently longing to make sleep come by virtue of saying the words.

I went to a Buddhist temple for the first time with my paternal grandparents and learned how to bow before the golden Buddha, from standing, to kneeling, to pressing hands and forehead to the ground, then turning the palms upward and lifting the hands slightly, and I felt myself fall away in my focus on the movements. This genuflection was almost identical to 큰절 (keunjeol, big bow), performed for elders and ancestors, except 큰절 does not include the palm turn and lift. During this trip I performed 큰절 for the first time at my father's family graveside plot in the mountains, paying my respects to ancestors I had never met.

But back in the United States, we rarely saw family and did not attend church or go to temple. The only religious items in the house were an unused copy of the life and teachings of Buddha, a set of mala beads, and tucked in my pillow, a piece of folded up paper. I only knew it was for good luck and protection. Sometimes I would slip my hand inside my pillowcase and touch the paper as I fell asleep. Recently I asked my mother about it, and she said it was some kind of 부적 (bujeok), a paper talisman for good fortune, prosperity, and protection. Mine was a gift from a Buddhist monk who was a family friend. Derived from Chinese Taoist talismans and first used by Korean 무당/만신 (mudang/manshin, often translated as shaman), 부적 are usually drawn in red ink on yellow paper, using classical Chinese characters, esoteric symbols,

even the images of animals. Mine was black ink on white paper, and I
never unfolded it to see what it looked like, and eventually, I lost it. But
for years, I slept with a piece of monk-blessed writing.

I don't know what my 부적 looked like, but images of shaman's
부적 are available online. I am most struck by the esoteric symbols,
which are combined in visually striking patterns. Sometimes they
strongly resemble the Chinese characters they are derived from. At
other times, they are repeated, reversed, and otherwise broken down
until dissolving into beautiful but semantically unreadable swirls and
loops. These symbols are considered spirit writing, intelligible only to
the shaman, and feel deeply akin to asemic writing, a form described
by poet-artist Michael Jacobson as "a wordless, open semantic form of
writing that is international in its mission," "a shadow, impression, and
abstraction of conventional writing." The poet and multidisciplinary
artist Sam Roxas-Chua 姚 sees it as "words I believe we will never
have words for. That's asemic to me. A made-up script that is alive, an
inner frequency."

부적, from a photo by Ryan Berkebile

While I have not made asemic writing a part of my poetry practice, what resonates with me, especially in the context of poetry as prayer, is the feeling of openness and attuning to an inner frequency. Earlier I asked, "What do you hear in your stillness?" We often can be so swamped by the external demands of life that we become only reactive and continually outward-facing. To see what happens when we are still and receptive to our own hearts can feel like a terrifying prospect. But vulnerability is required for both prayer and poetry. In a way, the incoherent space we inhabit during grief is one of great potential. When our sense of self is shaken, we have to imagine new ways of being and relating to the world. But we don't and can't always live in emotional extremity. What are other ways to reach the necessary openness?

The forms of prayer and chant themselves can help foster receptivity. Something in the repetition of words and sounds can allow us to sink into a meditative state, where the mind quiets, and whatever has been waiting for the space to come forward into our consciousness can do so. An experience familiar to all of us, I think, is how unexpectedly meaningful thoughts can surface in the shower. Being absorbed in repetitive movement and focused on the physical self can allow us to slip into a meditative state without effort. I sometimes find that the preoccupation that happens while wrestling with form in poetry can similarly shift my awareness. When a formal problem preoccupies my most conscious thoughts, an unexpected line or image will emerge that leads to the true heart of the poem.

Cultivating openness doesn't have to require loss or stillness—motion, practice, even working with resistance can foster a state of attentiveness. Recently I have been trying to integrate Buddhist chant into my life and poetry practice. Visual poet Monica Ong introduced me to chanting "Nam Myoho Renge Kyo," a central part of practicing Nichiren Buddhism, based on the teachings of the thirteenth-century Japanese monk Nichiren. Nam can be translated as "devotion," and Myoho Renge Kyo is the title of the Lotus Sutra, a twenty-eight-chapter scripture from Shakyamuni, the historical Buddha, considered by most Buddhists to be his ultimate teaching. The heart of the Sutra is that all people have the potential to be Buddhas, and Nichiren believed that chanting Nam Myoho Renge Kyo helps bring forth our essential Buddha nature.

I don't know for sure what my grandmother was chanting those mornings in Korea, but I believe she was reading from the Lotus Sutra. Part of me finds it strange that I am attempting a Japanese Buddhist chant rather than a Korean one, but I am learning to listen to my inner self, which tells me that sometimes, our lineages are not continuous. That when direct lines of blood and culture are severed, we can find other paths of connection and seeking understanding. My interest in Anglo-Saxon after my grandfather passed was a search for grounding and understanding through the origins of English. I sought the same thing in Korean too, driven by the realization I had missed the opportunity to really speak with my grandfather, and started taking courses in Korean language. Even my current exploration of Buddhism can be partly attributed to longing for connection to my grandparents, all of whom have passed now.

A principal aim of Buddhist chant and practice is to answer the question: What is our Buddha nature? I don't know exactly, but the teachings in English of Korean Seon (Zen) Buddhist Master Seung Sahn suggest the answer lies with the don't-know mind. If we let go of the striving, want-to-know mind and instead empty ourselves into the fullness of living in each moment, we can become our most loving and compassionate selves. I find the idea of the don't-know mind resonates with eighteenth-century English lyric poet John Keats's idea of negative capability, the ability "of being in uncertainties, Mysteries, doubts, without any irritable reaching after fact & reason." The actions of chanting and bowing are a practice that can help us reach this state. Master Seung Sahn says, "'Ah, chanting—very good feeling!' It is the same with bowing 108 times. At first people don't like this. Why do we bow? We are not bowing to Buddha, we are bowing to ourselves. Small I is bowing to Big I. Then Small I disappears and becomes Big I. This is true bowing." The Small I, the self, bows to the Big I, which is our authentic self, which is our own best self, our inner Buddha, fully connected to humanity.

Something like this happens in poetry too, in the intense attention to language and feeling that writing requires. At first, it can feel like an insignificant sound, the voice of the I, a single self, but then the boundaries between self and word and world dissolve, and our consciousness becomes expansive. To pray, to invoke, to appeal, to believe that there is outward support for this opening up can give us the push to allow the Small I to dissolve, to be held up by a larger, divine connection. And even when we aren't praying, when we separate systems of belief from poetry, the simple act of writing is an act of faith. In the act of making with our words, in the act of poiesis, there is an echo of the belief that Word can make the world: "And God said, Let there be light: and there was light."

Rilke says, "Every angel is terrifying." But what if you are the angel? What if the power you are afraid to call upon and know is your own power? Consider the possibility that the outward address of poetry as prayer was actually an inner invocation, a tapping into our own divine and enlightened self. To be "pressed … suddenly against his heart," to be "consumed in that overwhelming existence" could be what happens when the Small I dissolves into the Big I, a divine alignment rather than a loss to be feared.

Permitting the loss of self reveals that we are permeable, that we are not separate from but entangled with our communities and surroundings, which means we can in fact transform ourselves and the world both. My grandfather may be gone, but in poetry, which I am trying to write in Korean as well as English, I can address him and speak to him as I never did when he was alive. Performing 큰절, knees and hands and forehead pressing to the ground, thousands of miles away from his scattered ashes, I can feel closeness to him. Simply reading with careful attentiveness, I enter into communion with another, broadening my understanding of myself and what words can do. What have I heard from my innermost self? That surrendering the singular I is not annihilation but an opening up, necessary to becoming our most expansive selves. That I can attend, I can tend, I can be tender and receptive to the world that was and to the world that is. That I can also visualize and bring intention toward a new and better world through the power of language. Together, what future can we call into being through our poems, our prayers?

prayer for healing

HYEJUNG KOOK

may you listen
to the wound
may you hear
in the red noise
of your pain
the sweet song
of a cardinal
a voice
of living flame
or the voice
of a loved one
may you trust
the inner self
that knows wholeness
that you are connected
you are infinite
you are loved
when you listen
may you hear
what you need
to heal
to live
to die
with joy

SACRED PRACTICES:
Rituals of Repair and Revision

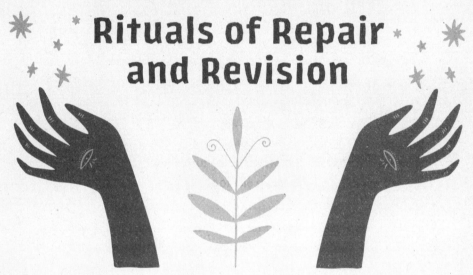

Revision as Mutability

AMIR RABIYAH

*In the process of telling the truth about what you feel or what you see, each of
us has to get in touch with himself or herself in a really deep, serious way.*
—JUNE JORDAN

In 2008, I joined on as a student/teacher/poet, or STP, at UC Berkeley's
Poetry for the People program. Poetry for the People, or P4P, is a poetry
as social change program founded by the late poet June Jordan in 1991.
It had been a dream of mine to work with June Jordan in P4P, but sadly
she passed away in 2002 before I ever had the chance. However, being
selected to be an STP was an honor, and I was thrilled to be a part of it.
Working with another STP, I was responsible for a small cohort, mostly
undergraduate students of color. All the students in all the classes would
meet for a lecture or a guest speaker, and then we would head over to
our classrooms.

I remember the looks of fear and anxiety on their faces on that first
day. I suspected they were scared of the unknown journey we were about
to embark on, of being judged, of failing, of revealing too much. These
were all feelings I was intimately familiar with. We created group agreements together, and my co-teacher and I agreed that this was not going
to be a writing space that was going to be competitive, violent, or cruel.
We would make space for them to show up as themselves. We would
hold one another accountable. As teachers, we would model vulnerability through sharing our own work with our students, and even our

own struggles with writing. We encouraged our students to strip away any unnecessary words as poets, something that June Jordan encouraged. We shared with the young poets examples of June Jordan's poetry, to demonstrate the importance of concise and clear language, and how language laid bare could illuminate the page, making your reader weep or sing.

As a child, I would often sit and write for ages underneath the avocado tree outside our house, in my bedroom, or in the hallways of my school, leaning against the lockers. I even wrote poems in chemistry class, as soon as I realized that the teacher really only cared about the students gifted in sciences. In those days, writing often poured out of me, and I did a much better job of snatching up those tugs of inspiration. Most of the things I wrote in notebooks, or even for school, I did not revise much. Nobody taught me how, or taught me why revision was so important. Aside from the lack of training in revision, I was overwhelmed with the sense of having to get it right the first time. I was raised mostly by the Arab side of my family, who left Beirut during the Civil War just a few years before I was born. The unspoken traumas of having to leave the homeland was a specter inside our house. As a result, there was always a pressure to keep up appearances, and mistakes were not an option. I internalized the belief that I was not allowed to make any errors, there were no rough drafts, no do-overs. Only that clean draft was acceptable, with perfect handwriting, free of whiteout and crossouts. If I dared write a rough draft, it would immediately end up ripped up in the trash can.

This pressure of perfectionism would follow me into adulthood. It wasn't until I started taking creative writing classes in undergrad that I was asked to revise my work, or that I learned that it was even an option for me. Feeling forced to revise often left me feeling lost, not knowing where to begin, or even how. I would be overwhelmed with a panic and anxiety at the prospect of it all, and I looked around at the other students who didn't appear to possess the same level of anxiety I did. All I wanted to hear from teachers at that stage was that it was okay to make mistakes, that it was good to write a rough draft, a first draft, a second draft, or even a third, or fourth. But many of these writing classes were filled with competition, and pretentiousness, leaving little room for traumas to interfere with the writing process. I found the same problems in my MFA writing program. There wasn't space for me as a queer and trans writer of color to name how these traumas from my childhood were impacting me in school. There was no space to name how the structure of the institution, methods of teaching, and curriculum reinforced white supremacy and were violent.

While in my MFA program, I began seeing a therapist. Over the years, I had gone through a number of them who moved on to other ventures or who weren't a good fit. When I found S, it was the first time I truly felt seen by anyone. She validated the anger, depression, and rage I was feeling. She made space for me, and she was the one who began to tell me that it was okay to make mistakes. At first, I was not able to fully internalize that it was okay for me to be imperfect, or that I wasn't somehow inherently bad. For a large portion of my childhood, my grandmother told me that I was unlovable, worthless, and *haram*. My father seemed to value my mind and rewarded me for doing well in my English classes. And so, I tried my best to excel in reading and writing, because I received affirmation that I did well, which I translated to love. To fail—it meant that I was unlovable. It meant that all the things my grandmother said about me were true, and it also reinforced the messages I got as a nonwhite queer and gender nonconforming person—so I had to get it right, the first time.

It would take me five more years at least to recover from the rigors of graduate school and consistent therapy to get to a place where revision no longer terrified me. It was my students in Poetry for the People who were my impetus. If I could have this compassion for them, why then could I not deliver that same compassion to myself? Years after leaving home, I still carried the abusive voices within me, telling me I was never good enough, yet at the same time expecting perfection. This realization is what inspired my journey of self-compassion. It is said that healing is not linear, and in my experience, this is absolutely true. My writing was directly connected to this journey, and if I felt stuck emotionally, spiritually, psychologically, or physically, that would show up in my work and how I approached revision. It wasn't until a decade after working with S that my first collection of poetry was published.

I've learned to approach myself more now with tenderness and care when revising my work. My anxieties around revision were founded in real traumas from my childhood, from being in white-dominated writing spaces, and from feeling lost in how to approach revision. If I share my work with others, I know that the feedback they give me may or may not be useful. I try to be open to what they have to say.

When faced with a piece that needs a lot of edits, I take deep breaths, I light a candle, slip my headphones on, and play some music—or if the birds are singing outside, I soak that in. I do what I can to calm my nervous system down. And then I turn inward. I turn inward with self-compassion and care, and I ask myself the hard questions. Is what I am trying to say here conveying my truth? Are there any areas where I could be more specific? Can I go deeper? Do I want to go deeper? How is this line or that line working? I often will delete parts that I feel are masking the essence of what I am trying to say, or trying to hide from more painful emotions. Instead of running away from my pain and fear, I run toward it, and hold it. I play with form and have fun. Sometimes playing with form, or making it appear different on the page, allows me to see certain lines from a different perspective. Even if this means that I return to the original format, there is liberation in breaking free of conventions. Other times, I will cut out entire sections and move them around. This is a practice that I use on a regular basis, because I notice that the flow can be improved if I rearrange a poem.

While doing these practices, I take deep breaths, I am gentle with myself, I take breaks. I tune into my body and my spirit, and I listen for the wisdom within me and from my good ancestors. That wisdom will feel like goosebumps, or a warmth in my chest.

I know now that just as healing isn't linear, writing and revision isn't either. It's messy, and tricky, and sometimes exhausting. But to revise is a gift and an opportunity to go deeper and to decolonize. It's a reminder that we don't have to be perfect in order to be loved, or even to survive under white supremacy. In fact, we thrive when we embrace our imperfections. Revision is a form of reconnection with our truest essence. It's taught me how to be more comfortable in my own skin, how to soothe the terror, and how to embrace transformation both on the page and within myself.

CREATING A PRE-WRITING RITUAL

Ritualists, witches, and spell-casters of all kinds know that rituals are important practices to help us enter sacred space, bend time, and tap into our intuition and power. Creating and following a pre-writing ritual can signal to your mind, heart, and spirit that you are stepping out of the mundane, out of daily life, and into a sacred, creative space. Taking specific actions, saying your intentions out loud, even just noticing your breath and breathing with consciousness can all help you move to a place where you are open to spiritual guidance, inspiration, and deep creativity as you write.

Part of the power of ritual is its repetition. With each repetition, the words become more familiar in your mouth, the actions or gestures second nature to your body. Every time you perform the ritual, you build on the power you generated before. Of course, the ritual will never be exactly the same: the time is different and you are different each time you enter into it. As you become more comfortable conducting your pre-writing ritual, you will inevitably find ways to build on it, or you will alter it to fit the needs of the moment. As the essays in this section point to, repetition and revision are both generative and healing. Continue to return to the ritual, to the sacred creative space, and observe what unfolds and what unfolds differently.

What that ritual looks like is entirely up to you. We suggest you keep it short and simple to avoid creating another excuse to put off or avoid writing. However, there is always a time and place for more elaborate, time-intensive rituals. Perhaps when you begin a new project, or when you are feeling particularly stuck. In those situations, you may want to do the "Opening the Channel" prompt in the "Additional Prompts" section.

Here are some options to create a ritual that's right for you:

★ Clear your space. That could mean closing all your apps, minimizing your browser, clearing or cleaning your desk, turning off your phone, sweeping the floor, etc. Again, don't use this as a procrastination tool—spend only a minute or two on this!

★ Gather physical manifestations or symbols of your writing or writing project. You might create a vision board to pin up where you can see it as you write, or create a small altar on or near your writing space that you can return to during your writing times. (You may want to revisit the "Ritual for Setting the Space" prompt in the Introduction for more ideas on making an altar). Before writing, spend a few minutes with this vision board or altar, really taking in the objects and symbols you have gathered.

★ Light a candle when you begin writing, and blow it out when you are done.

★ Take a few deep breaths, relaxing your muscles on the exhale, and sending energy to your creative center (wherever that is for you—sacrum, belly, heart, etc.) on the inhale. You could also envision your energy reaching out beyond your body and connecting to the energy of the earth, of plant allies, or well ancestors to support you.

★ Call in people, spirits, animals, ancestors, elements to guide your writing. Name them and ask them for specific or general help. When you are done writing, thank them and allow them to go.

★ Speak your intentions for your writing session out loud, or write it down and pin it to where you can see it as you write. This could be as simple as: "I intend to sit at this desk for thirty minutes and write at least five words." Or as specific as: "I intend to revise this poem to sharpen the central metaphor."

Begin by trying a combination of two or three and see how they feel. Then keep playing, experimenting, returning, and revising until you find something that feels right for you. And know that it will keep developing and changing as you develop and grow.

Practice:
Repetition and Return

TAMIKO BEYER

Every morning, my partner, our two dogs, and I set out into our neighborhood, which occupies the land of the Neponset tribe of the Massachusett people. Half a block from our home, we chat with the knot of
retired men gathered outside the coffee shop. We make our way down
streets lined with old brick factories on the banks of the Neponset river,
close to where it enters the Dorchester Bay. On a good day, we run
into the dogs' dear friend, a health-care worker making her way to the
trolley stop. We wave to the hair stylist through the plate glass salon
window and turn off the street. We greet a giant oak and beech shading
the field and say hello to mugwort as it makes its wild and steady spurt
to the sky through spring and summer. We greet wild roses by inhaling
their luscious scent and nod to the bees who crowd each other at the
lip of the blooms. When we arrive at the river, the creatures who live
there all or part of the year call to each other, and we call out to them:
herons, Canada geese, the white-crested duck who has somehow made
a family among the mallards, chipmunks, ospreys, plovers, kingfishers,
and eagles.

At the water's edge, I crouch down, take out my pouch filled with
home-grown herbs: sage, tulsi, rosemary. I offer thanks to the spirits,
ancestors, and past and current Indigenous stewards of the land and
river. I give further thanks to my ancestors, spiritual guides, and guard-
ians. I make prayers for the day, ask for blessings and protection for me,

my loved ones, and all beings. I set the dried herbs in the mud or afloat on the water. Patti and I exchange a few words of love and gratitude for each other.

Then, with one final glance toward the water, we turn toward home.

I have been practicing this morning ritual for five years or so, developing it through repetition and return. It began organically as we paused each morning to enjoy the sounds and sights of the river. We started to take a few moments to express gratitude, and eventually that morphed into prayers.

At some point I realized I ought to be making offerings for all the prayers I was making. So I started bringing plant allies as offerings, first from my stash of purchased medicinal herbs. When I started my garden, I grew plants for the offering and soon ritualized the acts of harvesting, drying, and blessing the herbs.

As for the prayers I say each morning, the words came to me over the years as I sought to be in right relationship with the land and waters, all the beings that reside in and on them, and the spirits and ancestors of this place on which I am a settler-colonizer. Meditating in the same spot day after day, practicing stillness and presence, I connected with words that felt appropriate to the place. Blessings came as the water flowed out into the bay, and words of gratitude arrived as the tide brought ocean waters upstream. Phrases accompanied the wind bending the river grasses or blowing across the frozen surface of the water in winter, acknowledgment of all the beings breathing, flying, swimming, and in stillness with the rhythms of the seasons.

These moments of prayer were not separate from the rest of my life. For example, after the 2016 US presidential election, I uttered Assata Shakur's words each morning as prayer, protection, and inspiration: *It is our duty to fight for our freedom. It is our duty to win. We must love each other and support each other. We have nothing to lose but our chains.* In the height of the COVID pandemic, every morning I named all the people I wanted safe from the virus.

And there are two simple phrases I repeat each morning, along with whatever else I am praying for. These have become sacred to me through this repeated ritual, morning after morning—a prayer and a spell for all beings as we live into the day ahead of us.

Early in my journey as a poet, I learned that one of the most important things is to show up on the page, again and again. It might be a cliché at this point, a familiar and sometimes maddening piece of advice to writers, but as a young person, it was revelatory. The teachers I found emphasized that the act of writing—no matter what happened to the specific piece of writing—was what made one a writer. Gail Sher, a Zen Buddhist and writer, in *One Continuous Mistake,* wrote of four "noble truths for writers," in which the fourth truth is: "If writing is your practice, the only way to fail is to not write."

I learned through experience that waiting to write until I was inspired or had a marvelous idea was a sure way to *not* write. I found that if I kept returning to the page, inspiration would also return with me—not every day, but enough to keep me going.

Following the direction in Julia Cameron's *The Artist's Way,* I showed up every morning to write three pages in my notebook, filling composition book after composition book with my very messy writing. I made writing dates for myself, carved out time each week to work on my poems. I wrote many poems—some very bad, some alright, and a few good ones. I revised and revised some more. In this way, I wrote a manuscript, revised it, and revised it again.

At some point I decided it was finished. Although I was proud that I had accomplished the feat of writing a book, I spent little time celebrating or honoring the work. Instead, I immediately began sending it out to presses, whether through first-book contests or during open reading submission periods.

I began collecting the rejection letters, which I knew was part of the process. The manuscript was a finalist in one or two contests, and I received a few encouraging notes from publishers. But a year passed, and then another, and I kept gathering rejection letters, until it became harder and harder for me to send the manuscript to the next publisher or contest.

All those years I thought I was living into the truth that to write is to be a writer. But somewhere in my psyche I still believed that publishing a book was the way to become a "real" writer. When it seemed clear my manuscript would not be published, I wondered what I was doing with my life and time.

And yet, slowly, I found myself opening my notebook again. Practicing. Writing new poems. At some point, I came to terms with the truth that the process of drafting and revising that first manuscript was part of my practice. I finally acknowledged to myself that the value of that manuscript was not its publication. The value was in the process, in the learning, in the discipline.

This is a slippery truth to hold within capitalism. From childhood, it is ingrained in many of us that work is only valued if it produces something deemed valuable. Inside capitalism, effort as practice is only legible in certain realms like sports or playing the violin. Everyone admires the athletes who run laps, lift weights, show up to practice twice a day. Or the pianist who spends hours playing scales, practicing their fingering, returning again and again to the same difficult five bars. But practice in other forms is not valued, seen, or understood in the same way. Somehow, we are expected to get things right the first time we do it. To do something badly and to return again and again to get better at it—this is rarely valued within capitalism and white supremacy.

But the thing is, writing poetry is very much like training to be an athlete. You have to do your push-ups—whether that's morning pages or revising poems that never get published. You have to return to the source, that creative spark and fire that called you to poetry in the first place. Maybe you take a break for a few weeks, or a few years. But if you return to the page, and you take up the practice again—that is what makes you a writer, a poet, no matter what capitalism or white supremacy says. Not the publications nor the accolades. The practice.

I love this quote from writer and craniosacral practitioner Susan Raffo about the practice of healing. "There is a reason we call it a practice because that is what it is, for the rest of the time we are in our work, we are practicing. There is no endpoint. There is no arrival. There is only practice." Healing, she tells us, is a continual doing, learning (and unlearning), honing. It is the same with writing poems. It is the same with ritual. Poetry and spellcasting both benefit from a continued process of being attentive to, learning from, and discerning inside both the process and the result of the process.

I begin a poem by letting words flow, ideas spill, images grow and morph and change. What happens on the page is messy. It is often boring and trite. And I keep going. Or I put it away and I return to it days, months, or years later. When I return, I cut and cull. I rearrange lines. I write new ones. I'm listening to something inside me—my brain, yes, and all the years of learning "how to write a poem," yes, but also the part of me that responds intuitively to the music of the language. I'm listening to the voice or direction inside me that is attuned to the spark of images, to the aptness of metaphors. I say it's a part of me, but it's also the divine or spirit being channeled through me. I am listening for that which is greater than me, that which I have invited in to flow through me and onto the page.

This process of revision through thinking and intuition is a lifelong practice. It requires developing and building the muscles we can call attentiveness and discernment. These muscles serve not just my poetry but also the rituals and spellwork I engage in.

I have been practicing writing poetry for more than two decades, but I have only been consciously practicing ritual work for a few years. I am a beginner witch, an apprentice, a novice. I am learning by practicing, and I find that my years of writing practice assist me.

When I create a ritual or do a Tarot spread, I trust that whatever I'm working on is also working on me. It's a process beyond the material realm, beyond my ego-driven consciousness. I've begun to realize that mostly what is required of me is discerning what arrives and recognizing signs and coincidences as messages or invitations into further work. I'm learning to trust myself and what I know intuitively, just as I know what image belongs or doesn't belong in a poem.

And I also know that I need to practice. For more than a year, I have been pulling a Tarot card every morning. It's a practice of learning the meanings—the traditional meanings, those that the deck creators assigned, and meanings that come to me. It's a practice in opening up to my own intuition, getting out of my head, and not obsessing about "getting it right." It's a practice in trusting that what I "know" about the card is in fact what I need in the moment, delivered to me in symbol and story.

Just as I believe that when I write, (on the best days) the poems are not coming solely from me but also from the channel that I open up, I also believe ritual and magic are mutually cocreated. My morning prayers at the river or my Tarot pulls aren't so much a petition to the ancestors and guides for them to make my prayers a reality. Instead, I am asking them to join me as collaborators, accomplices, coconspirators, or cocreators. I'm asking them to help me learn what I need to know in order to manifest what I desire. I'm asking for additional spiritual power behind my actions and energetic focus.

Writer and facilitator adrienne maree brown says, "what you pay attention to grows." The practice of repetition and return in ritual and in writing helps to hone and harness my focus on what I want to pay attention to, which in turn grows the power of that focus.

Through my daily walks to the river, I have come to learn that place better than I know any other place on the earth. I have become intimately familiar with the cycle of the seasons, the beings that visit or make their home there, the way the sun breaks over the horizon in the dead of winter or blazes down in the height of summer. The river has taught me how to pay attention, how to see something new every day. The river—and all the beings it supports—has taught me how to pray. It has taught me that the magic of paying attention need not be effortful. The repetition of visiting this place with intention and devotion has helped me feel myself as a creature belonging to this earth in a way that feels authentic and true.

And through my lifelong practice of writing, I have come to understand myself more intimately, and the world around me more deeply. By being attentive to the development of ideas inside myself and in the world through language, I become attuned to the interconnection between myself and all beings. Returning to the page again and again requires me to be in relationship not only with myself but with what surrounds me, seen and unseen. It sharpens my ability to discern, to hear, and to attend to what wants to come through, and it teaches me about time—its nonlinear nature, its vastness. The poem takes the time that it needs. The work develops in its own time. What I need to do is show up and keep showing up to learn what I need to learn.

This is what practice makes. Not perfect, but true. Not product but devotion. Not results but experience. And this, I believe, is the work of living, of writing, of ritual.

& I repeat to myself

TATIANA FIGUEROA RAMIREZ

I unstoppable
as the rose water marries
caribbean rum to become
holy.
the quartz crystal drowning
at the base of this homemade
agua florida hot to the touch & vibrating
ripples to circle the rim
of the bowl, of the glass.
of the jar that once housed
the fruit I left for Changó.

& I repeat to myself

I gorgeous
as the lilies burst to perfume
the air. their orange cores staining
my hands like a palm reader's fingers.
roses curve into daisies that lean
into mums. a bespoke bouquet blessed
by intent, while sunflowers reflect light bouncing
between the candle & the cross
& the carving of La Caridad del Cobre.

& I repeat to myself

I untouched
as I watch the wick coal
at my fingertips. flame flickering
from ocean to lava
from sapphire to sunset.
a single stream of smoke marks
the way to heaven as I speak
spirits into the room. broom
at the door. & I hear La Madama laugh.

LIGHTING FIRES, BREAKING CHAINS

Poetry as Praxis for Spellworking

LOU FLOREZ

A Conversation with Lou Florez, Lisbeth White, and Tamiko Beyer, featuring excerpts from the essay "Craft of Witches" by Lou Florez

Any text is the absorption and transformation of another.
—JULIA KRISTEVA

Proverb, they say, is the horse that sentence rides; in the same vein, sentence is the horse that proverb rides. If any sentence gets lost, we use proverb to search for it.
—CHIEF SOLAGBADE POPOOLA

I. Spellwork: Memory and Community

What if we ask: what do we give to the other instead of what do we take? How and what do we share?

Talking about sharing is talking about labor. Years of tending, cleaning, feeding, arranging, praying, constructing, listening, lifting, heaving, moving for elders, for communities, for shrines, for spirits, for myself.

Memory tries to create themes and narrative, to string together experiences to form a sense of continuity. Magic, on the other hand, is an eruption both into space and into self. It breaks open the possibility of limitless elegant solutions and dynamic, poignant change.

An experience of magic: what is a Southern Bingo Parlor.

Between six and seven, my aesthetics as a witch were in formation. I've spent a lifetime creating constellations: altars, workings, books. My home is inside the memories of my mother's purse. Memories of Tuesday, Wednesday, Thursday nights, sometimes in Catholic centers, sometimes at VFWs, sometimes in smoke-filled halls. Tables piled with charms, rabbits' feet, lucky Buddhas, troll dolls ... how do you name the magic of things held in hands, of prayers, rubbing, and breath? My magic is a continuation of these things.

Lisbeth White: Every time we read the work that you sent in, this image of the Southern Bingo Parlor keeps coming back to us as readers as an experience of magic. Can you talk a little bit more about how that feels, and why that became such a primary experience for you?

Lou Florez: The Bingo parlors in the South of the eighties—places in Texas, Louisiana, Mississippi, and Arkansas—were found in small Catholic centers or VFWs. They taught me the Medicines of centers and peripheries, spaces to observe how Spirit pours itself from one form as it empties itself from another, little hole-in-the-wall places.

In our parish, the monsignor was the caller and rumor had it that he fled from Germany at the start of World War II. Lives lived, peripheries and centers, Spirit pouring and emptying.

My mom would bring the biggest purse imaginable. And every freaking charm, crucifix, lucky Buddha, anything that anybody told her was gonna bring her luck, give her some inspiration, that was gonna bring Spirit down, she had. But it wasn't about the charm. It was about her connections to the people who gave it to her. Everything had a narrative, everything had a story, everything had a spirit.

She was also that person, that woman, who would go and just talk to people and sit with them. She curated inward connection—the relationality that exists between moments.

The Bingo Parlor was about her connection to her community, and being able to hold everybody within the space. She made connections with people who for no other reason would be together. But they would talk to each other and that was her witchcraft moment.

The whole magic of the Southern Bingo Parlor is the actual connectivity. Even though I might be practicing [spellwork] alone, the way that I practice is inherently connected to the ingredients, is inherently connected to the time, and the spirit of what's going on at that moment. Really looking at how am I actually engaging the living world, versus just it being a dead substance that I get to command or that I get to demand of, that I get to objectify.

II. Spellwork: Ecstasis at the Crossroads

I was once at a ceremony on a beach and we birthed an emanation of the sea tied to our experience of that location, that time, space, and community of ritual—a perch-building—a meeting ground through which Spirit can enter, land, and leave. A bird must consent to settle despite our callings. As medicine makers our work is to create the structures, these thresholding spaces for meetings to occur: crossroads. Scientists have described the lasting effects of human's detritus upon the planet by naming a new geological epoch. If divinities are known by their absence, what will be found in our remains? Toni Morrison said she used the "we" to invite the reader in, to acknowledge their home within the text. A spell or incantation are vibrating words that emerge centrifugal in its motion, resounding ripples of nature, transforming the we that decenters the Anthropocene and investigates the consent of Beingness.

Texting with the poet Dottie Lasky about poetry, ritual, and spellcraft for an essay I was writing and I asked her what a poem was. She said a poem was a combination of sounds like how abracadabra was a spell. Words elicit an experience; you create your own meaning that is always generative.

In Denver, between cigarettes and card readings, the author Selah Saterstrom spoke about contradictions, how sometimes a word

can hold its etymological antithesis. To cleave can signify to both
separate and bring together, depending on one's orientation. We
spoke about cards as texts and how their meanings are like punch
bowl scrying—the cards are a focal point for the mind to go still and
in that moment we allow them to speak for themselves. (If you ever
want a synesthetic experience, get out a Rider-Waite Tarot and
follow the blue ribbon starting at the Empress.)

LW: A couple of things are sticking out to me, as you talk about the bingo parlor. One is the relationality, because that's the piece that feels so counter to the way individualistic capitalist culture works, right? Even the relationship of the will to the materials used in spellwork.... The other is: in describing the bingo parlor, all the talismans, and the way folks are relating to each other—how are all these things different containers for these energies to move through? It makes me think of creativity and the arts as a form of container too.

LF: I would like to play and, just for this moment, imagine light as concept, as form, as language, as gesture. What inspires the crest of one wave to become the trough of another? I gather bits of myself in the works of Selah Saterstrom and Akilah Oliver. These are people that have inspired my processes of dissolution and coagulation—this idea of second tongued-ness—a moment where language as an everyday capacity goes away.

There are these happenings, there are these *ecstasis* moments, there are these experiences that are no longer translatable into everyday life. Something is so profound, you can't actually explain what's going on, and you're required to grow a new tongue, a second tongue, a tongue that expresses in Spirit what you can't say in the physical. I think that every witch that I've ever come across has had that moment.

What poesis is, is the investigation of that breaking, breaking into and out of, and also the in-between.

I think that whenever people talk about the crossroads, that it's not just a physical crossroads out there, it is the crossroads internally. It's a crossroads of when everything, every good, bad, everything in between the spectrum of life, and all the magnitude of that, is really open. And how do you settle in that? How do you really sit yourself there? We talk about the language of the crossroads as that place where anything and everything is possible—this idea of wildness or this idea of being outside of what we know as safety or security. I think that part of art, part of poetry, is that sitting there, trying to not try. It achieves itself. There is an achievement—whether it's on the page, whether it's spoken—of that ecstasis.

III. Spellwork: Opening to Spirit

I was once in Boulder, walking back from a crossroads after midnight with Akilah Oliver. We were discussing why witchcraft is never mentioned as a path to enlightenment. As a discourse, witchcraft is inexorably viewed through the gaze of colony, a refraction-like wave moving through matter at varying densities that obliquely deflects in the process. A witch once told me that part of understanding magic was to separate illusion from reality, the sleight of hand from a change in nature.

Black, Indigenous, and Brown bodies, female bodies, gender nonconforming bodies, trans bodies, working-class bodies, queer bodies are the historical perpetrators of witchcraft. One might ask, How can a body be primitive and superstitious, while threatening, powerful, and able to upend reality? My investigations center on how traditions hold and celebrate their people. How can they support thriving?

The practice of liberation magic is a magic of transgression, a magic that divests itself from the spiritual narrative of the colonizer by saying that my relationship to spirit, my relationship to my body, and my relationship to the world is outside of the gaze of consumption. I am talking about a politics of emancipation. How can a working simultaneously address a personal need while combating real-world oppression? How can a love-working address the intimate desires of the heart while displacing the patriarchal, sexist, misogynistic, heteronormative, racist narratives of what love is framed to be? If, as witches, our intentionally designed altars and conscious magic are not responsive to the intentionally created systems and infrastructures of oppression, then what are we doing and what are we working toward?

Tamiko Beyer: That's such a beautiful image, or a beautiful description of what creation is. I think both poetry and spellwork are about that creation. I'm wondering, are you drawn to poets and collaborating with poets because of this? I'd love to hear how you ended up discovering that you had this kind of connection with poets and poetry, and that magic and poetry are so aligned.

LF: Whenever I read [use divination], I engage a way of looking that isn't just the narrative, but really looking and seeing what is, versus what is just the story. What I believe this way of looking or divining offers to poets, writers, and artists is a place to really engage the spirit of a creative entity, and how it wants to speak, outside of the ways in which you try to make it speak on the page or in the spoken word.

I had the honor of reading for Selah Saterstrom as she wrote *The Meat and Spirit Plan,* and the questions that arose weren't necessarily about narrative but more around what the spirit of a character might want to say. And how do we inquire about that spirit? Selah took her own work and wrote, but that was our collaborative moment—actually talking to that spirit of the phrase or the character of the line, and allowing it to really speak. That's what both witchcraft and poetry do for language: it breaks the confines, and breaks the syntax. And I also think that magic helps us re-language syntax for us, reorder it.

I do a lot of collaboration because I believe part of the theory work and part of the practice work of magic has to be about bringing this information to the people. There's such a poetry on the street. There's an inherent poetry simply in the way people express themselves. And so, for me, it's an undervalued art form because it's ephemeral. But why do we not think of a poem like we think of a dress, like we think of a beautiful piece of art? Listen, it's like there's no access to believe that we're smart enough or valuable enough. The work of imperialism and capitalism is gigantic.

TB: I've been thinking about that a lot lately, actually. And about how powerful our magic needs to be because it's like centuries and centuries of such powerful magic of imperialism and capitalism and white supremacy.

LF: But we existed before all that! And that's the beauty of it. There are so many ancestors who did not live in that world. And that's how we get to channel it. We don't have to step back there. We actually get to bring it forward.

RITE OF THE VIOLET MOON

Offered by Lou Florez

This exercise is part of a larger volume of collaborative work with Dorothea Lasky from WitchCraft: A Happening—a writing and ritual experience in celebration of the full moons. We craft each lunar investigation by researching both Indigenous and modern naming conventions and divine each theme and its associations through the lens of what can create the most poignant experience for our community.

Violet is a color of light at the shortest wavelength within the visible acuity of the human eye, and lies between blue and invisible ultraviolet on the spectrum. Aboriginal Australians are one of the first cultures to create the pigment using crushed manganese and hematite as colorant for painting the body during ceremonies and medicine-making. Tyrian purple, symbolic of wealth, royalty, and the connection to the divine and ecstatic experience, was created by the Phoenicians as early as 1200 BCE from the mucus secretion of the hypobranchial gland of the cochineal sea snail. In classical paintings from China, violet represented the transcendence of duality, the uniting principle creating the ultimate harmony in the universe.

The Moon's revelatory journey through the night sky is a prominent cultural symbol across the human experience. From associations with fertility, wisdom, astral and invisible travels, romanticism, and visionary experiences, the moon's mystique represents the visible-unseen, the sublime, the voice that is always speaking under the surface.

Violet Moon associations: diamonds, third eye, seashore, cheer, emotional thriving, memory, delicacy, holding hands, humility, light, shrinking, royalty, tchotchkes, invisible spectrum, and radiate.

Immersive Magics

The Arts of Spiritual Bath-Making

INGREDIENTS:

2 cups sea salt

½ cup Violet Flowers

⅓ cup Althea Root (Marshmallow)

⅓ cup Coltsfoot

⅓ cup Purslane

⅓ cup Star Anise

9 Bay Leaves

a splash of olive oil

rose water

1 soup pot

1 pouring vessel

2 tealight candles

strainer

(herbal substitutes: Mugwort, Dittany of Crete, Angelica Root, Rue Seeds, Artillery plant leaves)

Meditate on the conditions that you would like to court into your life using the Violet Moon Tea associations. Create a simple nine-word phrase that can be imbued into each ingredient because this will be the anchor for the work. Using a large soup pot, fill it with water and begin to separately add the salt and herbs into the pot. As you work with each ingredient, focus your energy and imagine them absorbing your intentions as you speak them out loud. Next add a tablespoon of olive oil and bring this mixture up to a boil. As it begins to boil, bring it down to a low heat and let it simmer for an hour. Take off the heat and cool it to room temperature. Strain the herbs and add the rose water to the remaining herbal liquid.

Stepping Through the Doorway:

The Rite of the Violet Moon

★ Bring the prepared bath into the bathroom. If using a bathtub, fill the bathtub with water and add herbal bath to it. If using shower, consider adding a bit of warm water to the mixture in case it has gone cold.

★ Light your candles and place them on two surfaces that are across from each other in order to create a space like a doorway. After you have your two candles lit, you will step through the space between them, as if they are a doorway, and thus step into your bath. Before stepping into your bath it is recommended that you do one of the following: make a prayer, state your intentions clearly, or recite an appropriate passage that inspires this work.

★ After soaking and focusing on your intent, you will want to move into the rite itself. Using your pouring vessel, you will pour water from your head or neck down seven times. If you wish to preserve your hairdo, pour from the neck down. I highly recommend pouring from your head down. You will pour your water and enact the rite in the following manner (note: you will repeat this set of movements nine times in a row):

    ★ From the head or neck down, you will pour the water down the front of your body.

    ★ Each time before you pour the water, you will think of the qualities and conditions you want to court and cultivate in your life. For some people this takes the form of a prayer; for others it is enough to just allow the words to form. Either way: Say it out loud!

★ As you will do this series of gestures nine times in a row, you may say the same prayer each time or you may say a different prayer each time. This is up to you.

★ After you have said your prayer and poured the water down the front of your body, put your pouring vessel down. Now you will make these specific movements: Starting at the feet, sweep the bath up your body, imagining that you are being filled with Violet Moon energy. As you reach the crown of your head, say "Violet Moon, I now invoke you."

★ To recap, this will be the pattern, nine times in a row:

  ★ Prayer and pouring water down your body

  ★ Putting down the pouring vessel

  ★ Brushing up from the feet to the crown of the head while imagining yourself filled with the Violet Moon.

★ When you have completed the rite and have air dried and put on clean clothes, you will dispose of your bathwater. In the olden days, people bathed in portable tubs outdoors, and to dispose of their bathwater they would simply tip the tub in an eastern direction. Because most of us no longer bathe in this way, you will fill your pouring vessel with bathwater, and this will represent all of your bathwater. After you have your bathwater sample, the rest of the water can be let down the tub to drain.

★ You will dispose of your bathwater by sprinkling it around your bedroom, starting in the east, the direction of new beginnings and inspiration.

★ It is typical to make a recitation as you sprinkle the water in the form of a prayer or other improvised words. A simple "Let it be" or "It is done" also works fine.

Spell for Safety

CHING-IN CHEN

*for the trans and gender-nonconforming students walking the stage at
Lavender Graduation*

Maybe it was you learning to walk home

cross-wise, your own safety valve.

You, who trained a tongue

chosen name, listening for reflection to speak

back. You, I'm calling you,

grew yourself at argument's end,

slept borrowed and burned. Who

filled in space of the wisecrack, who

emptied the sidewalk, who

cleared the toxic table.

You breathed down your own street, rose tall, stitched. Built your own table, lit candles for the living who couldn't make it back. The invitations, the city, the hauntings and the hatchets, the you, the you, the you walking home safe, opening the door, setting the table for company.

ELEMENTAL ECOLOGIES, SPIRITUAL TECHNOLOGIES

Iniġluu—perpetually

JOAN NAVIYUK KANE

As a poet, as an Inuk, I am habituated to seeking patterns and connections, to associate and imagine, to center images, to translate experience into embodiment. I write poems as proof of life and continuance, and to protect life and continuance. I do not write out of an imagined relationship to earth and ocean. I do not write to escape the capitalistic banality of city life. I write because language brings me back to and affirms the significance of the arctic in my life, though I must live my life outside the arctic. And it is only through survival here, in Massachusetts, that I will be able to return to the places I know and the places that help me experience poems before I begin the process of writing them.

My childhood was filled with the near-constant refrain of "I want to go home" from my Ugiuvak (King Island) family. The migration of King Islanders to places distant from our ancestral homeland is not new to our people, but the seemingly permanent multigenerational displacement from our homeland because of systemic and structural changes initially dictated by various colonial governments is relatively recent: no one has inhabited Ugiuvak for more than a few weeks at a time in the last half-century. I understand now that when my family says, "I want to go home," we also mean, *"I want to go into another time."* Not the past, necessarily, perhaps the future—or some other temporal designation. "I want to go …" is the operative anaphora, the repeated wish, the unwavering assertion. Despite such direct insistence, and having myself finally traveled to Ugiuvak, I understand the implied undersong that presents now in the broader #LANDBACK movement: "Home wants me to go there." To collapse the distance between home and me—

Mind, bring me home. Home, restore our bodies to you. Senses, send me home. Home, fill my mind with the life of our land. Hand, fill the page with memory—

Anyone who has been in the arctic during the summer months registers the land's redolence—sagriq (Artemisia tilesii), aluk (Empetrum nigrum), *and* saayugraq (Rhododendron *subsect.* Ledum)—to name but a few of the wild plants that thrive and support the boreal ecosystem. These plants flourish during the endless white nights of the north—a time of perpetual light when darkness does not fall for months. One collects sagriq to heal any number of wounds, to promote good health, to cleanse. The dense evergreen growths of aluk yield black berries that sweeten after the first frosts in early fall. A potent tea can be steeped from the leaves of saayugraq, to ease pain or bring death.

From my earliest memories, these and other minuscule, pervasive, and intricately complex plants informed my relationship to the land, distinguishing its sustenance from that afforded by the life of the sea and ice. And they grew too on the few acres in the Matanuska-Susitna Valley that my parents acquired for a few brief years in a late-1970s land lottery. There, they had erected a wall tent that served as our year-round camp—a place to spend time on the land, away from the Muldoon neighborhood where they rented a two-bedroom apartment close enough to the city bus line for my mom to get to and from work. They let me call this place "Magicland" even after they let the site go, having found it an expensive and unsustainable liability.

My earliest memories too are ones of proximity attuned by the intention of my grandmother to equip me to sense the world clearly— the odor of my grandmother's home, so close that everything she prepared for nourishment could be guessed with accuracy from the sleeping bunks against the outer walls. The sense (before I was judged to be old enough to wander East Anchorage alone) of being pulled along in a bright orange sled by my mother from Delaware Place to Dover Avenue as an early snow fell and transformed the neighborhood's lawns into white fields of green stubble. The astringency of suraq (willow leaves) stored and served in the thickness of whitish-gold of mizaġaaq (seal oil).

In this way, I grew up in the city, but through nature and nurture I am wired for the land. An only child with many, many close cousins and relatives—so many that as my childhood bled out into an intense adolescence troubled by the constant dissonance between constructed environments and their consequences—I grew desirous of time alone, time on the land. My mom let me spend as much time as I wished outside, without restriction. I used much of this to get to know the woods that encircle Anchorage, and began to learn about every living thing around me: collecting plants, pressing ones I did not know how to use, even though my maternal grandmother had long since passed—

Elders have long told me how emphatic my grandmother was about young people maintaining fluency in the Inupiaq language. After being orphaned in the 1918 flu pandemic, Jesuit priests removed her from a Catholic mission school, arranged a marriage for her, and sent her along with her two sisters (also with arranged marriages) to Ugiuvak. There, she taught for many years, running a bilingual Inupiaq-English preschool. Her insistence upon plant knowledge would have been an extension of her belief in the vitality of traditional knowledge. She was a healer—quick to catch symptoms of brain tumors and of autoimmune diseases—and midwife too. My mother carried over her mother's practice of pressing plants to aid in learning about them. I wonder how much the range and viability of these plants from my childhood and adolescence have changed in response to all that continues to change—

I remember fidgeting at the foot of her hospital bed as a priest read her last rites, accidentally raising the head of the bed by stepping on the controls meant for nurses at the bottom of the bed, comprehending the solemnity of the moment enough to remember the physicality of my mortification. How familiar that sensation remains, how recurrent—

How, when I found myself in my mid-twenties with a thesis manuscript due at the end of a protracted five years of graduate school, I remember falling in despondent supplication to the floor of my Manhattan apartment, asking my ancestors to give me some sort of sign about what I was doing with my life. What mattered? What did I know—

These questions helped me muster up the minimum page count, to work my way out of the years of silence and writer's block that had been exacerbated by racist and hostile graduate advisers (one who handed me a copy of a John Haines book I found to be replete with cultural appropriation and colonial violence. Another who prided herself on fashioning a school of "feral" poets out of Ivy League students while at the same time suggesting that, given my profound sense of unbelonging in the type of commercial MFA program, I might do best by dropping out). Somehow, in the muggy swelter of my first-floor apartment, just down an embankment that ran downslope from a West Side highway ramp, nearly tranquilized by the fragrance of a massive linden tree that grew from the crest of the embankment, I found my subject: the images and symbols, the minute facticity, the ars poetica of tundra verdure.

I wrote one long poem about four of the five disasters that Inupiaq of the Bering Straits region have survived throughout millennia—an earthquake/eclipse/flood/famine brought about by a year of two winters and the 1918 flu pandemic. I wrote another poem about some of the plants I knew to give life. Another was about placing spruce boughs in sea water for the purpose of getting herring to lay eggs upon them. Yet another about suraq—willow (Salix) leaves—rich in salicylic acid. These plants, and the images of them fixed in my mind, sustained me, figuratively and literally. I found my voice to be alive through living memories of plants. I found a way to reach back through the turbulent family history that had placed me in the position of being beholden to life through language. Had I not written those poems, I would have defaulted on my student loans, would have moved quickly into the kind of life I have managed to keep at bay—one without poetry, without having had the means to travel to Ugiuvak, without children raised into our language and with knowledge of our lands.

In subsequent years and the manuscripts I have made through (or despite) them, I learned that I find my line when I can say the line as I write it. If I rely too heavily on language only to function as a kind of factual apparatus for an idea, a whole poem can veer off into linguistic or semantic complexity without using the duration of a line to carry emotion, perspective, sound, or lyric context. It stops coming to me as an Inuk and starts to feel manufactured. Sometimes I find that conversational language doesn't work for poems; I'm reaching for expression in a language that opens, through sonics, into other forms of meaning, or evokes possibility somehow through its utterance. Just as a working purchase on working English never resulted in upward mobility for so many of my family, in the last couple of years, living and working entirely away from Alaska, I have looked to the Inupiaq language in different ways: I have spoken it with my sons in our home, but less with my other family simply because I am with them less. I've been thinking about the ways in which the Inupiaq language affords my poems a different kind of interiority and versions of public and private and plural selves. I think I'm working out how translation figures in my work, and not just between languages, but in the act of pressing my cognitions through words and sounds.

My writing is also reactive, somehow—informed by worry and observation. Compelled by sovereignty. Even living outside of Alaska—in the city I am sovereign, raising my sons alone without the traumas that characterize life in Anchorage (systemic and structural violence against Indigenous women)—the once predictable seasons upended by climate change remains a central preoccupation of my work and dominates my relationship to place. And I need to be in conversation with my environment in order to write.

It has been important to me to refer to histories and knowledges, personal and shared, because as a poet, I feel they contain things I need to bring before readers in order to reflect upon the ways in which events and contexts of the past have shaped survival of any kind. My work is in conversation with histories and places and the lives they sustain that have a claim on me; they remind me I am not alone. My understanding increases when I remind myself how little I know and how much I can consider things more closely.

Is it possible that my poems (and in particular my poems that take as their subjects the embodied sovereignties of botanicals moving through their seasonal cycles at entirely out-of-sync-with-typical times) are forms of escapism? That they give me a way to lose myself in the intricacies of life that go on without me? Or do these poems place me in conversation with my ancestors, who observed the same plants, attentive to cycles, terrain, abundance, destruction?

I've neglected my practice as a poet in the months of the pandemic. I've taken too few walks. I've not moved through successive elevations. I've harvested little, though one day last June I collected linden blossoms with my younger son to steep into what he called a healing potion. Healing, perhaps, from the multiple traumas we left behind in Alaska, and protecting us from COVID. His father had him and my older son (just thirteen) fly to Alaska and back home to me in Cambridge in April of 2021 a few weeks shy of my older son's first COVID vaccination. I'd asked him to collect new spruce tips for me—the tender, bright growths at the ends of spruce boughs—and to gather saayugraq. I almost asked him to bring back a handful or two of the sagriq I gathered from the slopes of Ugiuvak on my first (and only) trip there in the summer of 2014. He would see my mom on his visit; she stores the plants in her freezer. He brought nothing to me.

I wonder if I will get around to making a tarot deck with images of arctic plants in place of the usual cards. I wonder if I will ever be willing to return to Alaska, to find my strength in the land and inua itself, or whether I will remain afraid of the pollution of the place. How triggered I am by the people who inhabit the land there, how problematic for me that so many non-Indigenous know how much we retain of the entire ecosystem.

I wonder too if I wrote the poems I did about Alaska because I knew I would lose my relationship to the place itself, that I would lose my home, that I would have to start over, with nothing, keeping my sanity for the sake of my sons as we wandered the streets of Cambridge, furnishing a mostly empty apartment we'd moved into in June 2020 with things those who were fleeing the city in the still early days of the pandemic saw fit to trash on the street. That I would find some perspective in the poems I wrote of the land, of the life that I found there.

I know that my poems about the land, ice, and sea are related to narratives of culture shock that Inuit know well, to narratives of disruption and cultural change. I know that I look to birds, to plants, to geography as a way to inform and calibrate my sense of pain much more than I look to these catalogs as a source of healing. My life and memories are indebted to entire ecologies that have sustained my people for millennia.

Mind, bring me home. Home, restore our bodies to you. Senses, send me home. Home, fill my mind with the life of our land. Hand, fill the page with memory—

WRITING HOME: BODIES

Who Are Your People?

My people is brackish water, salt marshes, tree moss, fish & grits, holy
    roller baptist praise, speakers of tongues,

healers through Sound, laying on of hands. mothers of mothers of
    mothers of mothers, cool hands on my forehead,

my people is standing stone, crossroads, keening, gatherers of Grace,
    constant and true.

     —GINA BREEDLOVE, from "Who Yo People Is" podcast,
        hosted by Sharon Bridgeforth, Season 2, Episode 27

In this prompt, you will invite your people into a simple list poem.
As the essays in this section explore, your people are not just the
humans in your family and community. Your people are also all the
beings and the land that you are connected to.

* Begin this prompt in front of your altar, perhaps the one you
  established in the opening ritual of this book. Take a few deep
  breaths to settle into your body. Reacquaint yourself with the
  objects you placed there. Remind yourself why you chose them.

* Create a sacred space or container in which to do this work.
  You can call in the corners if that is in your practice. Or light a
  candle or incense, burn some herbs, or simply say a few words
  out loud, inviting in any beings or energies you want to call.

* Close your eyes or soften your gaze and take three long, slow
  breaths. Ask yourself, who are my people? Who is precious
  to me? With whom do I want to be in deeper community?
  Whom do I want to protect? Whom do I want to protect me?

★ Invite in any or all of these:

- ★ the land and places from which you come or that you feel most connected to

- ★ beings of whom you are a continuation and with whom you are in community with, including ancestors

- ★ essences that inform you, guide you, envelop you

- ★ qualities you resonate with

★ When they arrive, welcome them with love and a generosity of spirit.

★ When you are ready, write down who arrived. For this prompt, consider keeping this a simple list poem. You could also use the list as a starting point for a poem that explores one or two of your people in more depth.

★ When you are done writing (for now), take a few more deep breaths. Thank all of your people who came when you called. You might want to listen for anything else they may have to say to you in this moment. Then, release the sacred container: close the circle, blow out the candle, or simply say: "Thank you for your support, love, and guidance. You are welcome to stay, or free to go."

A Korean Orphan Undergoes Catholic Training for Future Poets

SUN YUNG SHIN

One time in Sunday school, we took a field trip somewhere (another church? A Christian supply store? A museum? I wish I could remember) and our host, a middle-aged man, white, told us with good cheer that it was physically impossible for Jesus Christ to have been nailed to the cross through the palms of his hands, that the nails would have ripped right through his flesh and bone because the weight of his body would have been too much. Instead, he told us, pointing to the inside of his wrist, Jesus of Nazareth's crucifiers would have had to pound the thick iron nails through his wrists, in between the radius and ulna bones, in order to actually keep his body on the cross.

Every time I've seen a crucifix since then, I've thought of this man's delight at telling us this secret. (What about the stigmata? What about the saints whose palms bled because of their piety? Why wouldn't it have been their *wrists* shedding tears of blood?) How many times had I genuflected and crossed myself and entered the long dark pew and sat and looked up at the gigantic crucifix on the front facing wall of the church and contemplated Jesus's torture, suffering, sacrifice, and death? (The prominent crown of thorns, the long hair, the ribs and stomach muscles, the fresh and bleeding wound on the right side of his torso, the tendons of the outstretched arms, the legs, one ankle in front of the other, the feet, also pierced by a single iron nail. His upward gaze to his maker, his father, who had sacrificed his only son—for our terrible sins.)

What kind of human offerings could be equal to the extraordinary, visceral sacrifice of a demigod, the Lord's only son sent to live as a mortal among lowly human beings? We contemporary Roman Catholics in the late twentieth century in the suburban middle west of the United States didn't sacrifice any goats or bulls or lambs, let alone our only son, as Abraham was prepared to do to Isaac, as he bound him to an altar, ready to cut his life from him. But we tithed. We confessed. We consumed the body and blood of Christ. And we prayed.

We were reminded every Sunday and before every supper that God required poetry, from memory, as proof of our loyalty, his omnipotence, our dependence on him for that which kept us from starvation, our sins, and our salvation:

Our Father, Who art in heaven, hallowed be Thy name; Thy king-dom come; Thy will be done on earth as it is in heaven. Give us this day our daily bread; and forgive us our trespasses as we forgive those who trespass against us; and lead us not into temptation, but deliver us from evil.

The repetition of words: *in heaven, in heaven, thy name, thy kingdom, thy will, day, daily, forgive, forgive, trespasses, trespass.* The alliteration: *heaven, hallowed, kingdom, come, done, day.* The consonance: *name, come, done, heaven, us, trespasses, lead, deliver, evil.*

I learned in church that even the capitalization of letters were important, and God and Jesus were not *he* and *him* but *He* and *Him.* I learned that God is male and he chose a son for his glory, not a daughter. Mary was not blessed among *all,* but only among *women.* It was not her *mind* that was sacred, but her womb, and its fruit. I learned that Mary would not necessarily be present at our birth but she might be there at our death.

Hail Mary, Full of Grace, The Lord is with thee. Blessed art thou among women, and blessed is the fruit of thy womb, Jesus. Holy Mary, Mother of God, pray for us sinners now, and at the hour of death.

The stressed syllables at the beginning of each sentence lend this prayer a confidence, a solidity. *Hail. Bles*sed. *Ho*ly.

My parents encouraged my reading habit, but there was no poetry in my house as a child. My parents did not read books or literature, listen to classical music, attend plays, listen to scholarly lectures, but we went to church, which was book, literature, music, plays, and lectures all in one. And prayer, therefore, poetry.

The one poem visible in our house was a cross-stitched rectangle framed and hung to the side of my bed.

Now I lay me down to sleep,
I pray the Lord my soul to keep.
If I should die before I wake,
I pray the Lord my soul to take.

Aside from the first line, which begins with a firmly uttered *"Now,"* the poem is in iambic meter, a simple AABB rhyme scheme, and all mono-syllabic words.

Naturally, probably like every other child with this prayer on their wall, I was more than occasionally possessed with the cold dread that I would go to sleep and never wake up, with the likelihood of my soul going with God under question.

This prayer trained my child's mind to internalize the supplicatory power of poetry. To *cast* a spell means to *throw* a spell, and I felt that I was attempting to cast these words up, up, up to God, wondering how he would hear me among all the other children also casting their poems to Heaven.

If words could save my soul, words must be important. These prayers were a future poet's training ground.

Every Sunday from 8:15 a.m. to 9 a.m., my family and I sat, stood, and kneeled in the second-to-front pew of our church, St. Cletus Parish at 600 West 55th Street in La Grange, Illinois. We used to attend St. Barbara in Brookfield, but their service was longer. Our priest during my whole childhood was the outgoing, down-to-earth, Irish-accented, and joke-cracking Father Charles G. Gallagher, who had been ministering to our congregation since 1971 and who retired on January 2, 1990, the year before I graduated from high school and moved away to Boston for college. In his obituary on December 31, 2012, readers such as myself learned that he was ninety-three years old and was a former paratrooper of the 11th Airborne Division, Korean War Veteran.

The church was only twenty-four years old when I, about one and a half years old, arrived, wearing a hot pink hanbok and white rubber shoes, at the O'Hare Airport in Chicago on a warm June day in 1975, accompanied all the way from Seoul, Republic of Korea, by my escort, Mrs. _____, a Christian missionary and wife of a minister, whose ministry included escorting Korean orphans-now-adoptees to their new (almost but not always) white Christian families in America.

Another soul for Jesus Christ. I was to grow up for the next sixteen years in a suburb of Chicago called The Village of Brookfield; no brooks or fields in view, but it did contain the "world-renowned" Chicago Zoological Society, aka the Brookfield Zoo at (North Gate) 8400 31st Street. The Chicago Zoological Society, founded 1934, is a private nonprofit organization that operates the Brookfield Zoo on land owned by the Forest Preserves of Cook County. The Zoo, along with the Field Museum of Natural History in downtown Chicago, is primarily where I learned what a human was and what a human was not.

As a Korean adoptee, I harbor the knowledge that I was essentially randomly chosen—available at the right time—to be sent to a family of strangers in a foreign country who didn't speak my language and didn't look like me, and was to leave everything that would have been my familial and cultural inheritance behind. My adoptive parents told me that they didn't request a girl or a boy and would have been happy with either. They already had a boy, a white child, born September 11, 1971, in a nearby suburb, that they had adopted domestically, so it turns out they were pleased when they found out they would be receiving a girl from South Korea.

Our adoptive parents were Polish American and Catholic (mother) and Irish and German American and Catholic (father). Their extended families were and are Catholic. I grew up thinking most of America was Catholic. I just assumed, and no one really told me differently, that everyone grew up getting a cross of ash smeared on their forehead on Ash Wednesday and watched their mother fold the palms and tuck them into the gold crucifix on her bedroom wall. I figured most of America spent an hour or so every Sunday morning on their knees with their hands clasped together, thinking about angels, Heaven, Hell, and praying for Jesus to wash clean the stain of humanity's sins.

As a Korean American, I'm always tracking the parallel histories of my two countries, one that saw no future for me and two hundred thousand others, and one that sees me, on a good day, as a model minority, and on a bad day as a parasite, and every day as a foreigner.

As a lapsed Catholic, I no longer pray every day, or every Sunday. As a poet, I am always waiting for a prayer to arrive inside me and turn into a poem.

The older I get the closer the past seems. Time seems to keep folding forward on itself, bringing me nearer to ages before. Events from the nineteenth century seem painfully recent, because we are still living in much of the ideological and political world created by our "founding fathers."

I've returned to Korea five times as of this writing, and would have gone in 2021 because two of my poems were featured in the Gwangju Biennale "Minds Rising, Spirits Turning" held April 1–May 9, 2021, but due to COVID-19, air travel wasn't deemed safe in February and March, so much of the exhibition and events were shared online.

The poems in the Biennale are from my third book of poems/essays, *Unbearable Splendor,* and are titled "Autoclonography" and "Replication"; they are certainly spellwork, gestures of conjuring.

My poem "Replication" briefly alludes to the Binding of Isaac story, or simply, *the Binding,* הָדְיקָעָה, from the Hebrew Bible, Genesis 22, in which Abraham is commanded by God to bind and slaughter his son Isaac on an altar on Mount Moriah, הְרוֹם, as he would a lamb, in order to prove his loyalty to God, and which he proceeds to do, but is stayed at the last moment by a messenger from God who says, "Now I know you fear God." Abraham looks up from the altar and sees a ram and sacrifices it instead. This is a story that was told and retold to us as Roman Catholics, and my childlike literal interpretation was that it was a proof of God's cruelty, harsh demands, and even masochism (had I known that word at the time). The story remains illuminated and preserved in my child's mind's memory as the promise that he *can* and may well take everything away from even his most devoted. It also taught me that if you hope for mercy, for a reprieve, you had better behave as though you are willing to do as you're told up until the very last moment, or you won't be believed.

All of my poems are in some ways prayers for and to the missing and lost children of this world.

Those orphaned, abandoned, neglected, and murdered.

The missing girls, future women, of the world who were never born because of sex-selective abortions and infanticide in favor of boys, future men.

My strongest poem would be a spell to find them and heal them—and myself. My most powerful spell to cast would be to find my Korean family and stitch us back together with magic, some amalgam of English and Korean, but more, a spirit language that transcends space and time and holds the seeds of transformation.

A Christian missionary brought me to America, just as missionaries brought Christianity to Asia.

According to the *New World Encyclopedia*, Catholicism took hold in the Korean peninsula in the 1600s by way of China:

> *The Roman Catholic Church began to develop in Korea at the beginning of the seventeenth century, brought by Koreans who had met the faith and been converted in China. They also brought translations of the scriptures from China, and the strong and dynamic Catholic communities were led almost entirely by lay people until the arrival of the first Catholic missionaries from France in 1836.*

In Korea, with official persecution beginning in 1791, the 1800s saw thousands of Korean Catholics killed:

> *The Catholic community suffered major persecutions in the years 1839, 1846, and 1866, producing at least eight thousand known martyrs, killed for following a false religion. Among them were the fervent Korean priest Andrew Kim Taegeon and the Korean lay catechist Paul Chung Hasang. The vast majority of the martyrs were simple laypeople, including men and women, married and single, old and young. The members of this group of martyrs have been canonized as saints, with feast day September 20. Currently, Korea has the fourth largest number of saints in the Catholic world.*

Twenty-nine percent of South Korea is Christian, so there's a chance that even if I had grown up with my Korean family, or even just mother, I would have been a Korean Christian. I would have learned the Lord's Prayer in Korean, the Hail Mary in Korean. I might have memorized the verses of Genesis in Korean, and been occupied by the power of the word of God just as I was as an American child, listening to mass in English with inclusions of Latin, Hebrew, and Greek. Or if I had immigrated with my Korean parents, it is statistically likely that I would have been a Korean American Christian going to a Korean church in a metropolitan area where Korean immigrants settled.

Or, both as a South Korean citizen or an immigrant, I might have been Buddhist or not really religious at all. Less likely, but theoretically possible, I might have chosen to be initiated into a lineage as a mudang.

As a Korean American poet with many spiritual lineages, many kinds of prayers and poems in my inheritance, I believe everyone has access to the spellcasting power of words, that no god or gods own the power of language, nor should any person or group hoard or dominate others with its transformational magic. We have to be careful, because words can create worlds. Words can separate light from dark. Words can harm or heal.

Let us take these prophetic lines from Hebrews 4:12 and know that our words can be and do the same spellwork as we write, speak, and cast our poems:

For the word of God is quick, and powerful, and sharper than any two-edged sword, piercing even to the dividing asunder of soul and spirit, and of the joints and marrow, and is a discerner of the thoughts and intents of the heart.

If the word of God is like a sword that divides and dismembers, and healing is a return to wholeness, to connectedness, then my poems are like prayers against God.

They are but feeble ephemeral spoken words, mere breath through the doorways of the throat, mouth, and if written or printed, then bonded to the surface of thin sheets of pressed wood pulp, barely visible if turned sideways, their black ink marks invisible gazed at from the side, too thin for the naked eye to perceive.

How do poems heal?

By binding us to our own insignificance, and by that, reminding us of the embodiment of our oneness with everything in our universe. We are made of the things of the world, the matter, the empty space, the dark matter. We are 64 percent water. We are as trees, we are as rain. Our blood carries metals around our body. We must consume various amounts of certain minerals to survive. We are copper and cobalt and iron.

We are both sacrifice and altar.

During his lifetime, and at different periods of his life representing different stages of his growth in his faith, Abraham made four altars. It was at this fourth altar that his sacrifice of Isaac was staged. In my earlier summary of his story, I left out the fire, and the knife. In Abraham's time, only burnt offerings were made to God. Before Abraham bound Isaac, he placed wood on top of the altar, and then bound Isaac and placed him on top of the wood. He reached out with his knife.

The knife was to separate Isaac from his life, and to bring Abraham closer to God.

The knife is God's word, and as a poet, I feel a bit like Isaac, an Isaac who has stolen the knife.

No, I cannot kill God. I would not kill my father, nor his fathers, nor anyone.

Perhaps each poem is more like a spell of undoing, but not in the way God intended, not his undoing. An undoing of his demands for obedience, for a wholeness cleaved only to him.

Yet God wins in the end. We are all undone. I "don't believe in God" and I'm "not religious" but my training is part of my *soma*, my shaping, my embodiment. Words come from the body and are received and perceived by the body, whether in ASL or in American English or Korean. When we are able to wield our own language, we fight the dissociation and violation of language used against us, to divide us from each other, our selves, and the rest of the natural world and cosmos.

Because Death and Birth Are of the Same Stream

TAMIKO BEYER

I set the table for three. Ladle the soup
into the blue bowl for her, the others, the ones
to come. Beside it, a small mirror,

and an ocean stone. Spirals of light
shine up from the glass—
my own face. Hers.

Evidence of her in my hair
drifting into grey,
the lines creasing at my eyes,

how I rest my curled fingers
against my lips as I listen
to stories etched in decades—

women who make magic rooted
in doorways and threshold
gardens. In my cupboard, a jar: eastern

white pine needles suspended in honey.
Here, the fish cake, here the bowl of white
rice. All day, the sun tried

to come through. All day,
it failed. Now, evening, and I
am her scowl. I am the slippers

on her feet scuffing
across the worn kitchen floor
almost a century ago, thousands of miles away.

Outside, the kindling catches fire
under the ofuro. Yellowing newspaper.
Humid bougainvillea blossoms drop

to the earth. I pluck
a splinter from my palm.
Another prayer bends its knees.

SUMMONING POWER AND CLOSING THE CIRCLE

Ain't Got Long to Stay

DESTINY HEMPHILL

Tarrying in the spirit on the maroon-cushioned wooden pews. Laboring in the spirit while gathered in the living room turned tabernacle. Rocking back and forth, side to side under the leaky roof of an old movie theater made sanctuary. It was here and here and right here that I learned that the matter of spirit (matter as importance? Yes. Matter as in substance? Yes.) was the flesh.

Stay with me.

The sweat that beads at the pastor's brow as he whoops. The tears that stream down my mother's face as she kneels in prayer. The peppermint that my godmother's fingers dropped on my tongue to keep my mouth busy with something sticky & sweet & thus quiet. The laying of hands. The anointing oil placed at the supplicant's temples, in each of their palms, in the middle of their forehead, that was fuel for that fire in the belly and in the bones. All of this a conduit, a lightning rod calling Spirit to come down. To dwell with us. To be with us for a while.

And once Spirit begins its descent, you never know when somebody will catch it. There is never *a* time, but all the time (as in God is good all the time, and all the time God is good). It might be during the choir selection before the sermon or forty-five minutes into the sermon or during testimony when Mother Webb shouts, *But babyy—don't you know I don't look like what I've been through.* (Yes, bless this Black aphorism. May it forever stay with me as an affirmation that material violence even when not registered as glyphs upon the flesh leaves signs in the psyche and spirit.)

You never knew—but there were signs. The hush. The trembling. The deepening rumble and creak of floorboards as we stomped in rhythm to *Steal away / steal away / steeeal away / steal away to freedom / I ain't got long to stay here.* The quickened rocking. The tip of tongue to the roof of mouth as though preparing for a babbling issue of tongues.

In the sanctuary, by the river where people would get baptized before it was poisoned. In Tennessee and Texas and Arkansas. Nestled in the lap of my mother when she wasn't preaching. Wrapped in a prayer cloth as a child to keep me warm. It was here that I learned that flesh, the elements, and Spirit are inextricably intertwined. How the earth & the aether, beyond letters, share so much. This is where I learned to read the signs. To make apparent the invisible. To divine.

To divine is to practice perceiving the imperceptible, to practice making a bridge between the realms of the material and immaterial. In some instances, that means making kinship with the invisible. Receiving a message for your neighbor while reading tea leaves at the kitchen table along with the nightly scripture. Tasting the clay, mulling its bitterness in your mouth, & knowing a drought's nearby. My mother hearing hunger in my voice by the way I say hello over the phone. Or my brother and mother offering an interpretation of one of my dreams.

In the dream, I'm holding a painting I did. And the painting has dozens of eyes. I show it to my friend Mars, and they tell me that they love the lungs.

Oh, well—that's easy, my brother says.

Yeah?

Yes, Mama says. *You're getting a new perspective. Breathing fresh air.*

Days after the dream but before the dream interpretation, in the waking world, I watch Mars & their band perform at a house show. There, Mars sings a song. It's called "Lungs." It has a lilting refrain of "Can you make a little space for me?" Days after both the house show and dream interpretation, I find my great-grandmother Nellie's death certificate on an online database. She died when my mother was eight after being hospitalized with uterine cancer, but the death certificate names lung cancer as the cause of death. Days later, another friend shares with me that in Traditional Chinese Medicine, lungs are the organs where grief resides.

And suddenly, my ribcage expands. Makes a little bit more space for this constellation of Black matrilineal grief alchemy that has been asking me to follow it. Been glimmering and following me. A new perspective. Fresh air, so cool, so piercing—tingling, twinkling in my lungs.

Stay with me. I won't be with you long.

In some instances, though, to divine is to make a covenant with, to draw nigh and forth that which has been invisibilized. The hidden. The obscured. The deliberately destroyed, effaced, subjugated. My great-great Aunt Lucinda knew how to read. She knew how to read the English language on paper, sure. But she also knew how to read geography, behavior, between the lines of what was spoken and left unspoken, her own intuition. So when her seventeen-year-old little sister, my great-grandmother Nellie, turned up missing, Aunt Lucinda knew that it wasn't because Nellie just up and left and ran off with "that old man." Aunt Lucinda knew that Nellie wasn't hiding but had been taken and kept away. And she knew that Nellie's new husband, a man old enough to be her father, was who had taken her.

After visiting his old haunts and not finding him, she decides to go to the general store, the only one for miles: He has to go there sometimes if nothing else for some bread or a bit of hog head cheese. Aunt Lucinda asks the clerk what day of the week he usually comes in, what time of day. She returns when he's set to return. Hiding among the trees not too far from the general store, she spots him. She begins to follow him through the forest, a little behind him and parallel to the path he is on. Stopping sometimes so as to make sure he doesn't feel her behind him, but always keeping him in sight until—she sees him enter the shack where he's keeping Nellie captive! Aunt Lucinda settles behind the brush and brambles, waiting. Waiting. Waiting for him to leave. Once he does, she scoots on her belly while whistling a melody she and Nellie made in childhood. She sneaks into the shack and retrieves her sister, who had been kept and hidden from her for weeks.

My Aunt Lucinda's divination intervened in the anti-Black, patriarchal, capitalist, ableist logic that obscured the problem of a Black girl in rural Central Texas gone missing as a problem. Making a covenant with the imperceptible, the made-hidden, the subjugated is no trifling matter, then. Especially when making a commitment to pierce beyond what structures reality, to reach for the possibilities beyond those structures and toward the survival of yourself and your kin in the material realm. In this way, I understand my Aunt Lucinda's practice of divination and intercession as located within a constellation of Black divinatory practices, or covenants made with that which has been subjugated.

From the initiating entanglement of 1492, colonial modernity spells a world carved out of subjugation and captivity via genocides of native peoples, seizure of land, and the theft and capture of Black flesh. In such a world, liberation is rendered invisible and effectively nonexistent on earth under colonial modernity's siege. Consider then the covenants made by Harriet Tubman, Nat Turner, and other freedom seekers (some of whose names we know, do not know, or have been hidden from us). Drawing from the stars, from dreams, from the fire shut up in their bones, freedom seekers insisted (and continue to insist) a collective manifestation of liberation as possible. And how did they transmit this divinatory knowledge? Through a multitude of ways, of course, including the divinatory technology of song. They sang songs, encoded with instructions on how to read constellations in the sky for signs of routes to liberation otherwise obscured on earth. They sang songs about in which waters to submerge themselves when in flight. Songs to lure each other to secret edges of the forest, those hush harbors where they could be with each other, practice the ceremonial survivances from across the Middle Passage, breathe with each other, and—another name for breathing together—conspire.

These songs are my ancestral inheritance as they code my own survival and being. Indeed, belonging to a lineage of oral culture, many of these songs that issued from my forebears' throats have issued from my own. And these songs, these flesh-spun spells, these choreopoems (blessed be Ntozake Shange) are embedded with instructions of where to move, how to move, and when to move in concert with your kindred to get free. As such, they have been infinitely instructive to my own poetry and ritual practice. Like how to make oneself a conduit so as to align flesh, language, and ancestors that include earth, elements, and stars? Yes, that. And like how to give attention to repetition as a site that focuses and accumulates energy, pushing it beyond the fold of the potentiated into actualization? Yes, that too.

What else? Like how to turn language into an edge at which to meet, breathe with each other, and conspire. How to signal to others where to meet to enact radical possibility and to craft mutual liberation. A poetics of invitation and echolocation—a poetics of our mammalian instinct, as Sista Docta Alexis reminds us, singing: *I'm right here. I want you. Here. With me. To live free.*

What else, what else?... These songs taught me to remember something about my own poems: that the magic of poems is not the intercession that the poems make as themselves. That might be and often is very little (and we would behoove ourselves to be honest about that). The magic of the poems lies in the signal, which tells us that an intercession is possible if we were to come and *do* together as called. But then how does one craft this signal that is significant, that pierces through the chatter of everyday logic in order to sound a call for elsewhere?

With the ingredients of association and metaphor, for one—the same ingredients that make poems and potions so potent. Working against the strictures of the English language, my ancestors widened the pockets of possibility by creating signals that worked precisely because of the multiplicity in meaning, the slippage and slipperiness, the excess. So, when we sang *hush, hush, somebody's calling my name. What shall I do? What shall I do,* we sang about that inevitable fate that is death, yes. We sang about becoming still. Still enough to feel the heartprick that salvation was awaiting—the one this world doesn't give and the one that this world can't take away. We also sang about the type of salvation via liberation made possible by our kindred on this earth and in a world that did take away our freedom. In this way, the question becomes more pointed: What *shall* you do? Will you go under the hush of night? Will you meet those kindred waymakers? Will you breathe with them, conspire? In so doing, my inheritance models for me how to craft a symbolic language that speaks to material conditions and also pushes beyond them.

Stay with me, now.

And what shall we do with a language so thick with interpretation and slippery in meaning? Shall we harness it as a magic of revelation or a magic of distraction? Or put another way: How can we discern when we harness our language to make kinship with the imperceptible, to make covenants with the subjugated? And when might we be in collusion with the powers that obscure, hide, efface, and subjugate?

It's true that in the same pews where I learned that the matter of spirit is the flesh, I witnessed a language of distraction under the ruse of revelation. Under such a ruse, patriarchy isn't the issue but a woman's "Jezebel spirit" or a queer child "possessed by demons." Under such ruses, it's not the violence of anti-Blackness and capitalism that we must resist but slothfulness and the generational curse of poverty self-cast by our refusal to give bigger monetary offerings. Such turns of language under the guise of revealing some transformative truth distract from how that pastor and their congregation collude with the powers-that-be.

And, outside the pews, aren't we confronted with how the magics of distraction and revelation are increasingly important? As powers-that-be simultaneously counter and distractingly parrot the same language we've devised to pierce through our oppression and reveal our liberation? So that, according to some, we can "decolonize" tech industries without decolonizing the settler colony that occupies the land that tech industries mine from? And that abolition of police and prisons doesn't mean to put an end to, but only to permit their continuation in a somewhat diminished capacity? Such turns of language under the guise of revealing transformation distract us from the structural underpinnings of continuing oppression.

It is also true, of course, that these magics of distraction and revelation don't always exist oppositionally but are often intertwined to some extent. Singing the line *I ain't got long to stay here* might distract the untrained listener into thinking that we are only chorusing about death, expressing a yearning to be reunited with the Creator, reflecting an uncritical absorption of a Christian eschatology that insists on the world's ending. And this distraction could be generative as the same line works to reveal and echolocate a warning of impending flight along with a confirmation that the world, balanced on its fulcrum of anti-Blackness, must end for *all* of us to know true liberation. Or consider riots and uprisings in the face of the police murdering Black people: Some try to dismiss these nonverbal choreopoems as a distraction even as they are revelatory, embodied language that unveils the present prioritization of profit and property over people while so generously unveiling the possibility of that restructuring.

So many possibilities for our commitments, so much discernment required.

Stay with me. Please.

Because it's here … It's here at this edge, this possibility that I'm calling out to you and to your discernment. Earnestly. Right here at this particular crossroads, under increasing surveillance, against the clamor of everydayness that tries to propel us into more of the same—I'm calling out to you to meet me. Trying to shape the words, the songs, the choreopoems that might seem like a matter of no import to the inattentive. Might seem like just another death chorus. But to you—it might be a whisper in a register that can only be registered against your skin. And with that heat of breath on your flesh, maybe you know ... maybe you know a surging chorus of aliveness when you feel it? Maybe you recognize the song of liberation gloriously stolen back by kindred? Whispering ... like ... this ... Can you catch it?

Stay with me.   Because none of this can stay the same. Breathe   with me. Conspire.   We ain't got long   to stay here.

WRITING A COLLECTIVE POEM

Remembering that disruption and bridging are practices toward creativity, this prompt offers a way to engage in both. In Kenji C. Liu's essay, he shares: "To write a new poem necessitates burrowing into multiple texts, multiple 魔rgins, and these texts write the new poem." We take this concept as an invitation for all of us to engage in a collective ritual of writing into something new from what we encounter in the world and with each other.

This is a group practice that takes time to gather inspiration and resource out in the world. Though we are guiding this into a specific timeline, allow for plenty of flexibility and spaciousness to adapt to the needs or ideas of the group. Magic often happens in unexpected openings.

★ Invite a group of comrades into this intentional treasure hunt. This group can be an established group of folks you work, organize, write, or otherwise engage in a practice with. You can also invite friends, family members, community members, new or old—whomever you would like to create ritual with.

★ Each person should designate a notebook or app to utilize for this practice.

★ For one week, each person will be on a treasure hunt for inspiration. Gather quotes, images, lines of poetry, and text (from memes, bumper stickers, tweets, wherever!). The sources are unlimited, but the criteria is to gather material and words that move one toward a sense of power, hope, grace, pleasure, or generativity in the world. Jot these down in your notebook or app.

★ At the end of the week, have each person select five quotes they feel most drawn to share with the group and decide when you can all get together to share your inspirations.

★ Have an inspiration sharing party! Set aside at least an hour (depending on group size) to share each person's top five treasures. Share and listen attentively to what moved each other about what was gathered.

★ Within your inspiration party, set aside about twenty minutes with the intention of crafting a collective poem using at least two treasures from each person. Allow instincts and intuition to guide you all! The twenty-minute time limit will support you in going with your inner senses. If, after reading the poem aloud to each other a few times, the consensus is to revise further, take a week to sit with the words before coming back to rework them.

★ Once the collective poem is complete, bless it together in whatever way feels best for the group. You may say something collectively like, "May these words bring us strength and grace," or "May the reading of these words uplift all who hear them."

★ State this blessing and read the collective poem each time this group meets, either at the beginning or ending of the gathering (or both!). Notice if or how the space changes by bringing these words together.

★ Play around with this practice in whatever way suits the group. It may be that the poem comes together around a specific theme that fits for a certain bit of time and then another round of treasure hunting is required to keep the poem fresh. The group may want to try looking for inspiration around a certain topic or idea, or even renew the source inspiration based on the seasons or the moons.

★ Let this practice evolve and shift as long as it feels it feeds you.

Wander, Weave, (Un)know, Re-member

EDITORS

There is a ritual for unwinding time.

It is not really something to be spoken of outside the ritual space itself. What can be shared is that the ritual involves a circular dance and that certain things occur at certain degrees of the circle. Energies pop. Beings are called forth. Folks in attendance will talk about it—it won't be hidden necessarily, but these vague details are all a person who hasn't attended the ritual themselves might get to hear. It will be talked about in a spacious and circular manner, all allusion and innuendo. Not quite a secret magic, but a private one.

This circular and allusory way of speaking about the sacred is a common practice in communities of ritual and conjure. It can be irritating and seem exclusive to some folks, as it's possible to take the lack of concrete information personally. But this can be a wonderfully endearing practice of respect toward the sacred—a passing down, for example, from elders who close their curtains on the nights of a lunar eclipse to offer the moon privacy in its own ritual. It points toward a way of honoring power when it has been summoned to dance with us: by acknowledging the not-known, the mysteries themselves, and opening room for them to breathe, to move about as they will in space and in time.

This is a practice we as editors hold in high regard. We believe in mystery. We believe in the potency of human intention to create. We believe Rita Dove when she says, "Poetry is language at its most distilled and most powerful." We believe this to be true about spellcasting too.

What this means, dear readers, dear writers, dear workers of words and magic and change, is this book is a living book. Much like the serpentine nature of language, the essays, poems, and rituals that have found their way to this book are shifting and pulsing with mystery. They are ready to show one skin, wind around one meaning, and shed into a new interpretation with each read. They are welcoming of revisitation and revised practice. They encourage and lean toward, "What if?" They like for us to skirt the edges of our knowing. To play there. Sometimes, to pray there.

The nature of this book remains somewhat ineffable because of this. We are happy to invite the not-knowing to dance with what we do know because we must at some point end the process of writing and editing, because we must somehow close the circle and release the spirits of these writings into the world. So here, mysterious friends, are the invitations of what we know offered alongside our serpentine-fashioned reconsiderations of the essays you encountered up to this point.

This is what we know: All transformation requires radical imagination. Radical imagination arises in a container that can shift, morph, and adapt to hold an ever-expanding shape. In this book, we remember how the nexus between ritual and poetry can be a sacred container to manifest change and transformation. This, among other gifts, is particularly evident in Tamiko Beyer's essay as she draws our attention to how a willingness to return, to repeat, and to revise can be a pathway to ritualized presence. This ritualized presence can open a space to be nimble in our process and responsive to our communities while remaining grounded in what is. We receive this gift too in Amir Rabiyah's essay as they illuminate how revision can be a transformative practice as we deepen our capacity to not only reimagine poems but how we relate to ourselves, our genders, our lineages, and our communities. Within this nexus, we can summon communal connection and a subversion of the isolation wrought by colonialism and capitalism.

Indeed, this nexus of poetry and ritual can be activated to unlearn a range of scripts enforced by colonialism and capitalism. If colonialism and capitalism teach us to only recognize linear temporality, to recognize only the living and Human as worthy of consideration, to recognize something or someone as valuable to the extent that they can extract or be extracted from—the writers here invite us into the possibility that poetry can teach us something different about to what and to whom and how we can give our attention. For instance, in "Enchantment," Lisbeth White explores how lyric moments as embodied collapses of space and nonlinear experiences of time can enchant us into recognizing and acknowledging a sense of Beingness that is more expansive than how we've been conditioned to experience space and time. Further, Hyejung Kook invites us to hold gently the intricacies of poetry as prayer as a way to attune to our inner frequencies and to practice receptivity. In this way, poetry might offer a way to lean into the spaces that cultivate what is generative and creative, rather than those spaces that rely on exploiting what is measured as productive.

In deepening the power-building possibilities of our attention, poetry can also attune our senses to the more-than-human and to the interdependence of ecology. Dominique Matti's essay "Articulating the Undercurrent" chronicles how both poetry and flower essence–making are practices that help her form vital, sacred exchanges with plants, animals, and her dead in the midst of a swirling undercurrent of what is here yet not there. Similarly, in this realm, Destiny Hemphill shares how an ancestral inheritance of spiritual and divinatory practices reveals how our material conditions and the immaterial, the earth and aether, are inextricably intertwined. Through these essays, we remember that in order to transform current structures, we need to access different ways of knowing and different ways of being. We remember we will need to collaborate not only with the living (human beings and nonhuman beings), but also with our dead, our ancestors, unseen forces, and what we might call the divine.

This is also what we know: poetry and magic are necessary tools in societal transformation. In this book, we receive the reminder that transformation may entail alignment with energy that includes other forms of Beingness and knowingness: call those elementals, call that intuition, call those ancestors, call those gods. Many creatives and healers, including transnational feminist scholar M. Jacqui Alexander, refer to this phenomenon the "fourth voice": an energetic other that enters a creative space and guides a painting, movement, or poem to that moment of unknown possibility. It is here that Laurin DeChae offers a mapping of what moves within, beside, and behind us on these road-opening paths when we dare to call forth liberation alongside a polyvocal chorus of Black women. It is here that Alexis Pauline Gumbs listens to those slower, humming frequencies, which allow us to be present to Black feminist survivals that pierce through the confines of the known as they are shaped by the infinitude of what is love and its kindred grief. Through the writings here, we receive possibilities. We receive serpent-scale glimmerings that guide us toward what we need to summon transformation.

And it is because of polyvocality and humming frequencies that we also know that summoning for transformation may invoke a vast and universal silence, a disruption that cracks open beyond language, as Kenji C. Liu braves. Or a place beyond words, a space of symbols and images, gestures and movement, light and shadow, moving, as Joan Naviyuk Kane moves us, between memory and what the body knows as home in the face of brutal displacement via ongoing settler colonization. Perhaps a space entered through poetry or ritual, the place of our deepest knowings, the place in which we know—and become, as Sun Yung Shin invites us to remember—divine.

In a spiralic dance, such disruption of language can help us know even more intimately that summoning transformation requires being deliberate in reclaiming our own voices as we seek to actualize what we have radically imagined. With Lou Florez's essay, we are guided to revisit poetry as ritualized multilinguality, what Florez refers to as "second tongued-ness"—where everyday language is insufficient and we must move to language that has a capacity to stay with liminality, which is where magic is potentiated. Such reclamations can allow us to embody our own potency and, in this way, create an energetic pathway for collective revolutionary power.

This is also what we know: The structures, systems, and dominant cultures of the US are not tenable. Built on rotten foundations of genocide and slavery, settler colonialism and imperialism, exploitation and extraction, they never served the majority of people and creatures on this land. Thus, the crises drawing our attention in this current moment—the climate crisis, COVID-19 pandemic, continued racial violence, and the accumulating economic violences inflicted on so many people under racial capitalism—are not new. But they throw in even sharper relief the reality that we cannot continue in this world built by unspeakable brutality, colonization, anti-Blackness, and its attendant capitalist catastrophes.

In this book, we've practiced recalling a world that makes space for, respects the dignity of, and promotes the thriving of all peoples and creatures. A world that honors and is guided by our ancestors. A world rooted in the deep wisdom, experience, knowledge, and liberation of Black folks, Indigenous people, people of color, trans women, trans men, nonbinary people, cisgender women, queer people, neurodivergent people, and disabled people.

This is what we know: We write in the lineage of various anticolonial histories that activate the spiritual, the lyrical, and the mystic in order to demystify the brutality of current conditions and to intercede and to intervene. (We give thanks to the Haitian Revolution; Harriet Tubman; the poets of Angel Island; the writers and singers of kundimans; Denmark Vesey; Black Arts Movement; the Civil Rights Movement; Ghost Dance; Standing Rock; and the global movements, uprisings, and revolts under the banner of Black Lives Matter). Rooted in this lineage, we believe we can use a poem as an activating ritual that helps us attend more deeply to ourselves, our communities, and our planet. To summon, to cast, a new world into being.

Perhaps we have not unwound time in this book (though at least one of us editors believes we did!), but we have begun to unwind story, and we have begun to unwind the limits of whose story, why that story, and how a story gets to be told. In doing so, we have sought to reclaim the immensely powerful tools of change we have access to: voice, imagination, embodiment, efficacy, and sovereignty.

This is a book to circumambulate, to wander around with not-knowing and re-membering. This is a book meant to offer tools, ideas, and practices to bring us all closer to transformation and liberation of ourselves, our community, and our world. This is a book to weave a tapestry of mystery and healing through the effervescence of poetry, the intentionality of spellwork, and the liminality of both.

This is a book for us. This is our invitation.

Poetry as Spellcasting

FOUND POEM COMPOSED OF
LINES FROM CONTRIBUTORS

This is how we enter

A voice longing over longer and longer distances to be heard

The spell is spinning around herself

Giving the name a cosmology

You, I'm calling you

What do you hear in your stillness?

Death ... on the tongue and nontongue of everything talking

Every word is haunted by its past and potential variations

Listen for the wisdom within me and from my good ancestors

What can receive all that afterlife of vibration as vibration?

& I repeat myself

A tongue that expresses in spirit what you can't say in the physical

Making a bridge between the realms of the material and immaterial

We are both sacrifice and the altar

We turn toward home

Home, restore our bodies to you

Line 1: Lisbeth White

Line 2: Alexis Pauline Gumbs

Lines 3 and 4: Laurin DeChae

Line 5: Ching-In Chen

Line 6: Hyejung Kook

Line 7: Dominique Matti
Line 8: Kenji C. Liu
Line 9: Amir Rabiyah
Line 10: Alexis Pauline Gumbs
Line 11: Tatiana Figueroa Ramirez
Line 12: Lou Florez
Line 13: Destiny Hemphill
Line 14: Sun Yung Shin
Line 15: Tamiko Beyer
Line 16: Joan Naviyuk Kane

ADDITIONAL PROMPTS

Opening the Channel

This prompt is to help you clear your energy before writing and is a beginning step to practice divination through writing. It's very important for this exercise that you be in a place that feels protected and safe, so don't skip the first step!

★ Set a special space for this practice. If you have an altar already, you can sit there, or use the guidance for setting an altar from the intro. Take a few minutes to call in any supportive ancestral or spiritual energies that feel right—you can call the directions, the elements, certain ancestors, or spiritual guides. Light a candle, burn some incense, and do anything else that helps you set a ritual space.

★ Take a moment and make a note of a specific topic or idea you would like to explore in your writing. Keep it simple! For instance, write down a word like "river," "skin," "green," or a phrase like "Justice is ..." "Fulfillment is ..." "Healing is ..."

★ Imagine yourself in a circle or bubble of clear or white light. This circle is like a fine mesh; **speak out loud** the intention that only vibrations and energies of the highest frequencies and with your good as their sole intent can enter into this bubble of light.

★ Once you feel this circle of light around you, take some slow deep breaths. As much as is comfortable for your body, breathe deeply into your belly and imagine the breath moving from the bottom of your belly up through your chest and throat, exhaling through your nose. Do this for three or four deep breaths.

★ On your next breaths, sense, feel, and imagine this clear or white light surrounding you is moving with your breath, flowing into you through your nose as you inhale, down the center of your body to your deep belly, then flowing up from your deep belly up to your nose as you exhale. Take a few breaths like this, allowing that light to gently clear your body and your mind.

★ Try to practice this clearing breath for at least three minutes, or until you feel a sense of calm, stillness, lightness, or ease in both your body and your thoughts.

★ When you feel this lightness, pick up your writing utensils and complete your opening phrase. Write as stream-of-consciousness and unfiltered as you can for five to eight minutes.

★ At the end of the five to eight minutes, take a few moments to just sit and come back to the breath. Place your hand on the crown of your head and anywhere else on your body that may feel good, while saying out loud, "This is the boundary of my body. I close the channels that are most healthy for me to have closed today."

★ You can end by thanking your guides and supports for their presence and protection, then putting your altar to rest in whatever way feels good.

★ You may want to go for a quick walk or stretch and come back to this writing whenever feels good. When you do come back, make a poem!

Both, And

In poetry and in spellcasting (as well as in life!), holding two or more apparently contradictory ideas at once can be generative and illuminating. This prompt uses Tarot or oracle cards to help you tap into that truth. You can also do this prompt by finding images that speak to you.

- ★ If you are using a Tarot deck, pull out the Wheel of Fortune, the Tower, the Sun, and the World. If you are using an oracle or other kind of deck, pull out two cards that speak to you in any way about change, transformation, or loss, and two cards that speak to you of stability, personal power, or completion. If you are not using any deck, gather four images that represent these concepts to you.

- ★ Arrange the cards or images in an order or formation that makes sense to you.

- ★ Spend a few minutes meditating on what the cards or images bring individually and in relationship to each other.

- ★ Now, write a poem that holds two contradictory ideas simultaneously, but doesn't name the ideas. You can use the following structure to get started:

Line 1: Describe a sound without naming the source.

Line 2: Bring in an animal.

Line 3: Write a line of internal dialog.

Line 4: Present an object in its entirety.

Line 5: Describe or refer to a death.

Line 6: Describe texture of a surface.

Line 7: Write a line of dialog that comes from a being not human.

Line 8: Evoke a gap, a leap, or a hole.

Line 9: Write breath into the line.

Poem-Spell for Blessing and Protection

This prompt is a spin on Aracelis Girmay's offering for the Poetic Justice Institute at Fordham University in 2021. The poem of inspiration for that prompt, "Glory" by Gbenga Adesina, is a wonderful inspiration to read for this prompt too.

Part 1: The Blessing

★ Begin by listing three to five people, communities, places, things, elements of nature, that pulse with a quality of being you respect, admire, and cherish.

★ Choosing one of these, begin writing a praise-poem in which you describe, as intimately as you are able, their aspects and expressions, incorporating the following guidelines:

    ★ Begin each line with a phrase of praise or love. *Glory of* (like the Adesina poem), *Blessed be, Praise to, Gratitude for,* are some examples.

    ★ Describe at least three aspects or expressions of what you have chosen to focus on.

    ★ Incorporate at least three to six senses available to you in each description: a sound, a taste, a physical sensation, a color, a scent, or an intuitive knowing (dream or memory).

★ Once you have written at least three praise-descriptions, or have come to a place where the praise-poem feels complete, feel free to choose another combination of a person, being, place, etc., and begin again, or move on to Part 2.

Part 2: The Protection

★ For this second part of the poem, being by reviewing the praise-poem. Seek out and pay special attention to the aspects and expressions of what you chose to focus on that you associate with strengths, joy, resilience, capacity, grace, love—any positive qualities this being, place, object displays.

★ Now begin writing a poem describing how these qualities may protect the subject of your praise poem from harm.

  ★ Again, choose at least three qualities.

  ★ Begin each line with either: *May [description of quality] protect you from ...* Or *Your [description of quality] protects you from ...*

  ★ You can be as general or as specific about who or what this quality protects from. It may be a general protection against all harm or ill wishes, or a protection from specific people, policies, or energies.

★ If you feel so called, combine your praise and protection poems together.

★ End the poem with a phrase of affirmation that works for you. *And so it is, Amen, So say we all, So mote it be,* etc.

CONTRIBUTORS

Alexis Pauline Gumbs is a queer Black feminist beacon of love. Alexis is the cofounder of Mobile Homecoming Trust, a living library amplifying generations of Black LGBTQ brilliance. Alexis is the recipient of fellowships from the National Humanities Center and the National Endowment for the Arts. Alexis is the author of several books, most recently *Undrowned: Black Feminist Lessons from Marine Mammals* and the forthcoming biography *The Eternal Life of Audre Lorde*.

Amir Rabiyah is a mixed-race, queer, trans, and disabled poet. Their work has been published in *Kweli, The Feminist Formations, Foglifter, Mizna,* and more. They are the coeditor of *Writing the Walls Down: A Convergence of LGBTQ Voices.* Their poetry collection, *Prayers for My 17th Chromosome,* was a finalist for the Publishing Triangle Award and an American Library Association Over the Rainbow Pick. Amir lives in Pennsylvania and is a diversity resident and research and instruction librarian.

Ching-In Chen is a genderqueer Chinese American hybrid writer, community organizer, and teacher. They are author of *The Heart's Traffic* and *recombinant* (winner of the 2018 Lambda Literary Award for Transgender Poetry) as well as the chapbooks *to make black paper sing* and *Kundiman for Kin :: Information Retrieval for Monsters* (Finalist for the Leslie Scalapino Award). Chen is also coeditor of *The Revolution Starts at Home: Confronting Intimate Violence within Activist Communities* and *Here Is a Pen: An Anthology of West Coast Kundiman Poets.* They have received fellowships from Kundiman, Lambda, Watering Hole, Can Serrat, Imagining America, Jack Straw Cultural Center, and the Intercultural Leadership Institute. They have worked in Asian

American communities in San Francisco, Oakland, Riverside, Boston, Milwaukee, Houston, and Seattle, and are currently part of the organizing core for Massage Parlor Outreach Project. They are descended from ocean dwellers and currently teach at University of Washington Bothell in the School of Interdisciplinary Arts and Sciences and the MFA program in Creative Writing and Poetics. www.chinginchen.com.

Destiny Hemphill is a ritual worker and poet living with chronic pain on land of the Eno-Occaneechi Band of the Saponi Nation (Durham, North Carolina). A recipient of fellowships from Naropa University's Summer Writing Program, Callaloo, Tin House, Open Mouth Retreat, and Kenyon's Writers Workshop, she is the author of the poetry chapbook *Oracle: A Cosmology* (Honeysuckle Press, 2018) and *motherworld: a devotional for the alter-life* (Action Books, 2023). Her poetry has also appeared in *POETRY* magazine, *Carolina Quarterly, Frontier,* and elsewhere.

Dominique Matti is a writer, a mother, a messenger, and plant worker. She lives in Philadelphia with her two children, her books, her candles, and her jars (of potions, roots, leaves, and flowers). Through creative practice, spirituality, tending the land, and listening, she ritually strives to situate herself in the long story. Her work centers Black mysticism, ancestral inheritance, liberation, loving, and recovery. When she is not writing or running after her children, she works as a diviner and maker of spiritual medicines. She looks forward to discovering what arrangements of words will populate the rest of her sentences.

Hyejung Kook's poetry has appeared in *POETRY* magazine, *Denver Quarterly, Prairie Schooner, Glass: A Journal of Poetry, Pleiades,* and elsewhere. Other works include an essay in *The Critical Flame* and a chamber opera libretto. Born in Seoul, she now lives in Kansas with her husband and two children.

Joan Naviyuk Kane is Inupiaq with family from Ugiuvak and Qawiaraq, and is the author of eight collections of poetry and prose, most recently *Dark Traffic* (2021). She currently teaches creative writing in the department of English at Harvard University, is a lecturer in the departments of Studies in Race, Colonialism and Diaspora and English at Tufts University, and was founding faculty of the graduate creative writing program at the Institute of American Indian Arts. She was a 2020–2021 Visiting Fellow of Race and Ethnicity at the Center for the Study of Race and Ethnicity in America at Brown University, and held the 2021 Mary Routt Endowed Chair of Creative Writing and Journalism at Scripps College. Honors for her work include a 2018 Guggenheim Fellowship, the 2012 Donald Hall Prize, and a 2009 Whiting Award. She raises her sons as a single mother in Cambridge, Massachusetts.

Kenji C. Liu is a visual artist and the author of *Monsters I Have Been* (Alice James Books, 2019), finalist for the California and Maine book awards, and *Map of an Onion,* national winner of the 2015 Hillary Gravendyk Poetry Prize (Inlandia Institute). His writing is in numerous journals, anthologies, magazines, and two chapbooks, *Craters: A Field Guide* (2017) and *You Left Without Your Shoes* (2009). An alumnus of Kundiman, the Djerassi Resident Artist Program, and the Community of Writers, he lives in Tongva territory, Los Ángeles.

Laurin DeChae (they/she) is an Aquarius sun, Sagittarius moon, and Gemini rising. A natural shapeshifter, time traveler, and space bender, they are researching the ways in which magical thinking creates novel pathways for healing in concert with the literary and artistic contributions Black women have made to spiritual investigations of interiority and its praxis. They are currently located in New Orleans, immersed in its hauntings and in conversation with its spirits.

Lisbeth White is writer and ritualist living on S'klallam and Chimacum lands of the Coastal Salish. As a writer, she has received awards, fellowships, and residencies from VONA, Callaloo, Tin House, Split This Rock, Bread Loaf Environmental Writers Conference, the Dickinson House, and Blue Mountain Center. As a healer and ritualist, she has been a facilitator of community-based healing justice workshops for social justice organizations nationwide. She is the author of the poetry collection *American Sycamore* (2022), winner of the Perugia Press poetry prize. She is certain our collective liberation is intricately tied to ancestral earth wisdom and firmly believes each of us has boundless capacity within to be our own wisest healers.

Lou Florez (Awo Ifadunsin) is an internationally known Bruje/Witch, Medicine Maker, Herbalist, Spirit worker, priest, activist, and artist who has studied with Indigenous communities and elders throughout the globe. His teachings and practice are grounded in prompting connectedness to the body through physical, emotional, spiritual, and environmental landscapes, creating living, dynamic relationships so we can become conscious of the inherent power available to us in every lived second.

Lou comes from the spiritual legacies of Latine cultural wisdom keepers, Orisha Priests and Medicine Makers, and Brujas, and his work promotes spiritual activation and social empowerment. As the executive director and cofounder of Water Has No Enemy (2017–present day) Lou creates transformational dialogues and intersectional allyship between social change makers and leaders, and Indigenous culture keepers and medicine holders. As a creative and author, Lou is celebrating the release of his first book, *The Modern Art of Brujeria* (Simon & Schuster, 2022), and his writings have been featured on *Remezcla* (2020) and *Bringing Race to the Table: Exploring Racism in the Pagan Community* (2015). He cofounded WitchCraft (2020)—monthly full-moon happenings comprising poetry and witchcraft experiments. As a Presiding Priest of Ile Ori Ogbe Egun (2021), Lou creates Orisha-centered fellowship, services, and programming rooted in liberative theology and practices, and is an Awo Orunmila, or High Priest in the IFA tradition.

신선영 辛善英 **Sun Yung Shin** is a Korean-born writer whose fourth book of poems, *The Wet Hex,* was published by Coffee House Press in 2022. Her poems have appeared in *POETRY, BOMB* magazine, the 2021 Gwangju Biennale, and in many anthologies, journals, and installations. She received her MFA in Creative Writing and Poetics from Naropa University. Her work has won an Asian American Literary Award and a Minnesota Book Award, and she has been awarded fellowships from MacDowell, the Archibald Bush Foundation, the McKnight Foundation, and elsewhere. She is the editor of three prose anthologies: *What We Hunger For: Refugee & Immigrant Stories about Food & Family; A Good Time for the Truth: Race in Minnesota;* and *Outsiders Within: Writing on Transracial Adoption,* as well as the author of two books for children. She is also a community healing practitioner, dream writer, Tarot reader, bodyworker with United Bodyworkers & Artists, trained biodynamic craniosacral therapist, and the founder of Tyger Tyger Jewelry. She's a member of YallaDrum!, an Arabic drum ensemble of New Arab American Theater Works, and is enrolled in a trauma-informed yoga teacher-certification training program. With Su Hwang she codirects Poetry Asylum in Minneapolis.

Tamiko Beyer is the author of the poetry collections *Last Days* and *We Come Elemental,* both from Alice James Books. Her writing has been published widely, including by *Denver Quarterly, Idaho Review, Black Warrior Review,* and *Georgia Review.* She has received awards from PEN America, Lambda Literary, and the Astraea Lesbian Writers Fund, and fellowships and residencies from Kundiman, Hedgebrook, and VONA, among others. She publishes *Starlight and Strategy,* a monthly newsletter for shaping change. She is a queer, multiracial (Japanese and white), cisgender woman and femme, living and writing on Massachusett, Wampanoag, and Pawtucket land. A social justice communications writer and strategist, she spends her days writing truth to power.

Born in Puerto Rico and raised in the mainland United States, **Tatiana Figueroa Ramirez** graduated with a BA in English Literature and is a VONA Voices Alumna, having worked with award-winning poets Willie Perdomo and Danez Smith. Tatiana primarily performs, teaches poetry workshops, and hosts events in the greater Washington, DC, area, and has also done so nationally and in the Dominican Republic at venues including New York University, the Kennedy Center, and the Howard Theatre. She currently works in the nonprofit sector providing free poetry programming to underserved students in the district and is completing her master's degree in public management to continue intertwining her community work with the impact of poetry. You can read her work in *The Acentos Review, Here Comes Everyone (UK),* and other publications. She is the author of two poetry collections, *Coconut Curls y Café con Leche* and *Despojo.*

ACKNOWLEDGMENTS

To begin: we acknowledge that we write in the lineage of various anti-colonial histories. We are indebted to the writers, spellcasters, revolutionaries, organizers, survivors, dreamers, and fighters who activated the spiritual, the lyrical, and the mystic in order to demystify the brutality of current conditions and to intercede and to intervene. We again give thanks to the Haitian Revolution; Harriet Tubman; the poets of Angel Island; the writers and singers of kundimans; Denmark Vesey; the Black Arts Movement; the Civil Rights Movement; Ghost Dance; Standing Rock; and the global movements, uprisings, and revolts under the banner of Black Lives Matter, as well as to Angela Davis, Audre Lorde, June Jordan, lucille clifton, bell hooks, Grace Lee Boggs, and so many, many more.

This book would literally not exist if it were not for the vision and enthusiasm of our editor Gillian Hamel. So much gratitude to you and all the folks at North Atlantic Books who saw the promise of poetry as spellcasting and worked patiently with us as we created a book from the seed of the idea.

We are also indebted to all the talented poets and spellcasters who generously contributed their ideas, writings, and poems to bring this book into being with us. This book is much richer, wiser, fiercer, and more magical because of your words and intentions.

We send our thanks to the folks who helped turn our initial ideas into powerful panels at the &Now Conference (shout-out to organizers Ching-In Chen and Amaranth Borsuk) and the AWP 2020 conference, including Tatiana Figueroa Ramirez, Kenji C. Liu, and Sun Yung Shin. And thank you to everyone who attended those panels and made the original magic with us.

We are grateful to the editors and readers of publications in which some of the poems in this book were originally published:

American Sycamore, Perugia Press, 2022 ("Awakening of Stones: Hypothesis" and "Awakening of Stones: Results" by Lisbeth White)

Origins Journal ("Spell for Safety" by Ching-In Chen))

"Poem-A-Day," poets.org ("February" by Tamiko Beyer)

Poetry magazine ("how we got our blues-tongue" by Destiny Hemphill)

Southern Cultures ("& the portal appears" by Destiny Hemphill)

Texas Review ("because birth and death are of the same stream" by Tamiko Beyer)

Tamiko is grateful to the people and spirits in and of the land that holds her, including the Massachusett people past and present. She gives thanks for the generosity and guidance of her care-taking, trouble-making ancestors. And to Patti Lynn for the poster, the playlist, and the magic—life is better with you.

Destiny gives thanks to Nellie, Lucinda, Mabel, Lymal and other ancestors whose names have been hidden but whose stories stay in her heart and underneath her tongue waiting to be unearthed. She gives thanks to her mama, her brother, Mars ee Woods, Sarah, Suquanna Rose, Amy Wang, and the close ears they keep to the divine.

Lisbeth extends her gratitude to the circles of magic-workers who keep showing her the depth and breadth of where our magic can go—most especially to Cresta White, Lena Moon, Tiffany Foo, and Makenna Berry Newton. And to Wayne, for the steady and the sweet.